Reflections and Memories

A Collection of Stories for Seniors

VOLUME 1

GENE HELVESTON

MANAGING EDITOR

ygl Your Good Life

Reflections
and
Memories

YourGoodife.org is designed for the millions of people who are nearing or already in retirement.

YourGoodife.org offers entertainment while fostering growth through conversation and community.

Visit **YourGoodife.org** and discover a variety of opportunities to explore and share your literary side!

Our motto is:

Live your life to the fullest!

When originally published online, these stories were accompanied by photos. To find the stories and photos, simply type the title of the story in the search bar located on the Chapbook page at:

https://yourgoodlife.org/chapbook/

Contents

Contents

Contents

Contents

Foreword

by Gene Helveston,
Managing Editor

When we started Your Good Life, our goal was to create a literary website *for* seniors that was created *by* seniors. Our aim was to have the content entertain and to also be a call to action, a call to participate. This book is proof that our aims have been achieved.

While the editors assumed responsibility for setting the tone for the site in prose, poetry, memoir writing, and journaling, our hope was that readers would be inspired to take up the challenge and submit their own writings. This volume is evidence that they have done so.

In a little over a year since YourGoodLife.org was launched, readers contributed fifty stories—and it is these first fifty posts that make up Volume 1 of *Reflections and Memories*. These short pieces, written by ordinary seniors, originally appeared in the Chapbook section of YourGoodLife.org.

At the end of this book, you will find short bios for each of the authors. When you read the bios, you will realize these contributors are not so different from you … and we hope that the words provided by these writers, many of who are publishing for the first time, will inspire and encourage you to submit your own prose or poetry. Everyone has stories and memories to share!

YourGoodLife.org is free. There is no membership fee

or advertising. We welcome your participation as a reader and, if your muse is stirred, as a contributor as well.

Please send your submissions in a Word document to: yourgoodlife84@gmail.com.

Acknowledgments

Like many accomplishments in life, this book and the Your Good Life website (YourGoodLife.org) are a team effort.

First in line for credit, and the person most responsible for what the reader sees in print, is Lynda Smallwood. She has been a steadfast, loyal, and accomplished colleague in this and many other efforts over a fruitful period spanning more than thirty years.

Mary Jo Zazueta, a skilled editor, writer, and designer, has guided our efforts in promotion, quality of content, and design.

Ashley Tengler designed the website with consummate skill. It is her efforts that make YourGoodLife.org attractive and easy to navigate.

The Board of Directors and section editors of Your Good Life contributed mightily to whatever success we have attained. In no particular order, they are: Rosemary and Bruce Hume, Memoir Editors; Margaret Hall Simpson, Poetry Editor; Sandra Hamilton, Promotion and Development Editor; Lynda Smallwood, Media Manager; Fritz Llalendorf, Copy Editor; Ashley Tengler, Website Designer and Digital Marketing; and Jo Lesher, poetry and Haiku.

Acknowledgments

Steve Still, retired Executive Director at Marquette, offered encouragement from the beginning.

Marylin Martin and Casey Maish made our first roll-out possible.

Michael McGinley offered invaluable advice; while Ashlie Burnett and Kelly Berger provided support.

Many residents at Marquette participated in focus groups and have been loyal readers. You know who you are.

Roger Myers, of Presbyterian Villages of Michigan, provided invaluable introductions and enthusiasm. Also providing support from Presbyterian Villages of Michigan were Sarah Grant, Mary Katherine Hannah, and Tom Wyllie.

David Ruffer, from Hoosier Village, gave good advice.

Guy Miller, Jack Baker, Lynda Smallwood, Lynne Lalendorf, Elizabeth Simpson, Jerome Joffee, Rosemary Hume, Ruth Hillmer, Suzanne Kenny, Martha Plager, and Lisa Sprunger helped launch the photo gallery.

I am sure I have missed some names, including the readers I have never met, and for that I apologize. Know we appreciate you and your support.

Gene Helveston, MANAGING EDITOR

Reflections and Memories

Peep Show

by Betty von Noorden

Accompanying your husband on a medical trip to Brussels can be a memorable experience. What occurred at the time of the Brussels' World's Fair turned out to be a little more than expected.

Many years ago, my husband, a Professor of Ophthalmology, and I, attended an international meeting of ophthalmology in Brussels. For budgetary reasons, we decided not to avail ourselves of expensive accommodations arranged by the Society, but rather to seek our own. What we had overlooked was the presence of the World Fair, bringing thousands of visitors who also required accommodations. After much searching, we finally located a spooky-looking Bed and Breakfast.

Our first disappointment was with the absence of a tub or shower, and the presence of a basin and pitcher filled with cold water. The next shock was of the toilet location, which was across a courtyard.

After dark, with flashlight in hand, I ventured out into the night. While I sat enthroned, I noted the small window was broken, and to my absolute horror, observed a prying human eye. I lost no time racing away, shrieking the entire way back. Oddly, no response from any quarter! Upon reentering our room, my husband, roused from his sleep, muttered, "Where are the cats?"

Was that all? No, my friends! An hour or so later, in deep sleep, we were catapulted out of bed as it had lifted and folded itself into the wall.

At 7:00 am, we sat in complete silence over breakfast of coffee and croissants.

Later that day, fortunately, we encountered a Brussels colleague who offered us sanctuary in his home.

The Vonnegut Name

by Beverly Heid

In business for more than 100 years, Vonnegut Hardware, a fixture in Indianapolis, was a vibrant business with talented team members, like the man described. Another developed the "panic bar," a safety device that allows a door to be opened from the inside while locked from the outside.

Many people in the Midwest are familiar with Kurt Vonnegut, the author. Indianapolis also had a popular company owned by Clement Vonnegut.

Ray Carmichael was my dad, who was instrumental in the expansion plans and promotions for Vonnegut Hardware. During World War II, Dad organized the Victory Gardens Campaign. They held a large promotion in the Coliseum. My sister Joan and I were preschoolers and sang for Governor Schricker at the show. We wore red-velvet dresses with pearl buttons. We had a big, gold **V for Victory** pin on our dresses. My dad promoted Victory Gardens. We had one in our backyard. He made a picket fence to enclose it.

Dad was very talented. He organized the Vonnegut Company Christmas parties and summer picnics. He did the promotions for all the new store openings. Vonnegut's had a downtown store that sold many things, including dolls for little girls. Dad designed and prepared all the advertising. This included TV advertising as well as newspaper ads. Dad won the Brand Name Retailer of the Year Award for Vonnegut's in 1951. He received a trip to New York City, where he received the Award for Vonnegut's. His memento included a home desk and chair (our daughter in Phoenix now has them), wooden humidor, and matchbox holder with a horse head inlaid. I have these items. We keep paper clips and rubber bands in the matchbox holder and new printer ink in the humidor.

Ray Carmichael was a talented artist long before he joined Vonnegut's. He was responsible for designing the store windows for the STAR store in Fountain Square. He also drew the promotional cards of the movie stars promoting the current movies at the Fountain Square and Granada Theaters. These are all in the past. Before his death at age sixty-three, he was painting show cards for small businesses to promote Christmas. Our nephew Ron Garrett and I have two.

Corn Toss, A Fun Sport for All

by Randy Trowbridge

Also known as "cornhole," "baggo," and "beanbag," corn toss has gone from being a tailgate event in the Midwest to a nationwide pastime with championship games covered on ESPN. It is also a favored activity at our retirement community.

The game has been played sporadically at our facility for at least five years. With increasing enthusiasm and a twice-yearly competition amongst four similar communities in the state, it has become a yearlong recreational activity. The accompanying commentary resembles that of professional sports.

The game can be played inside or outdoors. The corn-toss board is a 2' x 4' sheet of half-inch plywood with a six-inch hole centered nine inches from the top edge of the board. The board is supported by a 2" x 4" frame. The top of the board is propped up twelve inches from the ground. Two boards are positioned, opposite, facing each other twenty-seven feet apart. The boards can be constructed in a home shop or purchased at a local sports outlet or online. The cost of two boards and eight beanbags is between $100 and $200. If they are built in a home workshop, it would still be best to purchase official bean bags.

Opposing players may compete as singles or doubles. Each "round" of play consists of opposing players alternately pitching four bags. Each thrown bag that goes through the six-inch hole is awarded three points. Bags that remain anywhere on the board are awarded one point.

Official rules of the American Cornhole Association can seem a bit arcane, but local rules may be applied to fit the location and players. For instance, we have shortened the distance between boards from twenty-seven feet to twenty feet apart. We also allow players to "pitch" their bags from either side of the board. Official "cancellation" scoring gives one team the difference, if any, between the larger and smaller score at the end of each round. A round is completed when a singles or doubles team compiles 21 points. Our local scoring awards all points earned after each round. The first team to reach 31 is the winner.

Women and men compete on an equal basis. This makes the game a sport that can be a valuable social event for all people who choose to be involved. Youth, such as grandchildren, can play the game and, in some cases, can give a senior valuable pointers on technique.

Full-Time Camping in Retirement

by Joe Helveston

Life as a senior does not march in lockstep. There are alternatives and the following describes one.

After thirty years of camping experience, my wife, Nancy, and I believed we were prepared to transition to a full-time RV life. We sold our house and purchased a membership in a camping club that allowed us to camp for no cost after paying an annual fee of $480. The one stipulation was having to move to another campground every two or three weeks. The moving around gave us an opportunity to see other places and meet more people. Our primary goal was to stay in the northern states through the warmer spring, summer, and fall months and head for Florida before the cold weather moved in. This gave us plenty of time to see our children and grandchildren in Pennsylvania, Virginia, and North Carolina.

For those of you reading this who have experienced the camping life, you know and understand living close to people is part of the lifestyle. Perhaps that's why we are such a friendly bunch. The people who are less friendly will want to have greater distance between themselves and their neighbors. Not only the close space but also the respect we campers show each other seems to create a positive lifestyle. I'm not saying we are all a wonderful group of friendly people but there is one great advantage we have over the homeowner. Our home has wheels and our hookups are easy to disconnect. I've met people from different parts of the country and with backgrounds that ranged from a retired judge to a retired Navy Admiral.

In one of the campgrounds we stayed in I met a couple traveling with five children, two dogs, and a cat. They were in a thirty-three-foot travel trailer pulled by a pickup that was loaded with bicycles. The parents told me they home-schooled the children and the father worked as a computer programmer. The dad told me he especially enjoyed seeing the way the kids learned geography they could actually see for themselves. The example he used was the Grand Canyon and what better way to learn about it than to be there.

Traveling through the mountains of Colorado or the shores of the East Coast is an experience we all should have. This would help give us a better understanding of how fortunate we are to live in this country. One of my favorite states to visit was Arizona. From the deserts to the mountains I was always thrilled by the amazing sights. When our daughter and her family lived in Tucson, we spent most of a three-week vacation enjoying the area. Now that we are staying in Florida during the winter months this gives the kids a place to escape to when their weather turns cold and nasty. I sometimes wonder how we made it through the long winters of Northern Michigan. Actually, I do recall flying out to Sun City, Arizona, where Nancy's father lived. We usually went after the Christmas holidays. Being able to do the same for our children is a great payback.

Making new friendships is one of the big pluses of traveling through the country. When I walked the dogs for exercise and to do their daily jobs, people would smile and make nice comments about how cute they were. Then I would often stop and begin a conversation, which could last for thirty minutes or more. Some of those conversations would lead to an evening get-together. We would play games or talk about family or places we've been to. Finding the best attractions was made much easier when someone told you how great it was and how to get there or how to solve a problem with the camper. There was never a shortage of good ideas and sometimes not such good ones. You learn to smile and nod your head, telling them how much you appreciate their suggestions.

One of the projects we worked on before taking off on our full-time adventures was a musical show we put together to perform at the campgrounds we stayed at. We played nine different instruments plus vocals. The music covered show tunes, Irish, country, and ragtime. We made a little money and had a lot of fun. Some of the campers made decorative hanging lights and many colorful kitchen towels were on display throughout the campsites. One of our good friends repaired computers and I remember a lady in one of the Florida campgrounds cut hair. Most of the places we stayed at would have a one-day-a-month craft show or yard sale. One of the local farmers sold fresh fruit and vegetables every Saturday morning at a campground in Pennsylvania.

The holidays gave us a chance to decorate the camper with pumpkins and skeletons with orange lights for Halloween or red and green for Christmas. There was a contest to see who had the most decorative site. The place we stayed at during the Christmas holidays had a dinner with all the fixings for the whole campground. We had a spirited group of carolers who traveled around the campsites singing to anyone that opened their doors. Every Sunday was church service in the main hall. We played our instruments one Sunday and got some nice compliments. Living the camping life is an experience I will always feel good about. The friendships we made and experiences we had will be with us forever.

An Indelible Memory

by George Charbonneau

My father confirmed a strong memory that I have of an event prior to the first grade. It is my first memory from childhood. It happened when I was four years old and when you hear it you will understand why I remember it—or maybe you will know why I can't forget it.

I am not writing this story myself. I have a ghostwriter. I don't think that's so bad. A lot of famous people do it and get paid millions for stuff other people write about them. I am being paid nothing. So there.

I was living in Ormond Beach, Florida, and it was 1934. Ormond Beach is still around, and it is thriving. It was a sleepy small town then, between St. Augustine, the oldest city in the United States, and Daytona Beach, where stock car racing was born. I lived with my family, which is not only normal but mandatory when you are only four. I mention my family because my dad played a big part in this tale.

Today the green sea turtle is considered an endangered species and the government has strict rules to protect these gentle giants. Things were not so eighty years ago and that is why the following could take place.

It was summer, in the middle of the egg laying-nesting season. Giant green turtles weighing between 250 and 400 pounds and measuring nearly four feet long crawl up on the beach at night, burrow in the sand, and lay between 75 and 150 eggs that are about the size of a Ping Pong ball, not all that big for the size of the turtle. When finished, the mother turtle buries the eggs and crawls back to the sea. In about two months, the top of the nest mounds up from the stirring of baby turtles and dozens, sometimes more than a hundred newborns, each the size of a newborn chick clumsily scamper to the sea where they can live as long as 70 years.

Now comes my part. My dad took me down to the beach in the moonlight when a large turtle was nestled in the sand and in the process of laying her eggs. My dad said, "You bend over, George, and catch one of those eggs when it comes out."

Of course, when you are four years old, you do what your dad tells you because, after all, he is the smartest person you know. I stuck my hand under the back end of the busy turtle and caught one of the eggs. This act produced the most enduring memory of the event. I felt a squishy liquid surrounding the egg as it came out. After that, I dropped it and let the turtle do the rest; that is, bury it. When the turtle was done laying her eggs, the next most memorable thing happened.

They put me on top of the turtle and walked along as the turtle, with me astride, went back into the ocean. The men were knee deep and the turtle was getting ready to dive when they retrieved me.

Thanks, Dad, for creating quite a memory.

The Gardener That Could be Any of Us

by Bruce Hume (and G.H.)

There are different ways to enjoy your garden. There is no right way; just the best way for you.

Just about anywhere in the country, "Spring is here" by May 1st. Here, in the Midwest, we can claim to be about average temperature wise. The grass is greening, the birds are singing, and the redbuds are in their full but brief bloom.

How about you? Are you ready to join in the fun of this season of reawakening? By this, I mean, have you thought about a garden? How do I define *a garden*? If you have a small porch patio or even a windowsill that can hold flowers, you can have a garden. It doesn't take a big spread or extensive beds around the house and scattered in the yard. All it takes for you to have your own garden is space with some sunlight and a watering can.

To get started, you should know what colors you like, have a way to get the flowers home, and a project that fits your budget.

Traditionally, and by that I mean fifty or sixty years ago, this venture started at a nursery or garden shop. Today it can still happen there, but more likely, you will head for a big-box like Lowes, Home Depot, Walmart, or

Costco. There you will find hundreds of healthy plants in near endless varieties. Some will be in flats with individual plants in detachable green-plastic containers ready for planting or potting. Others will already be planted in pots six to eight inches in diameter or larger, ready for setting or for hanging. These plantings may be a single variety or a combination. My choice for starters: a purple petunia in a variety that does not require pinching, a Pericallis (never heard of it before) that I selected because of the unusual blue daisy-like flower with a white center, and a yellow African daisy. This beauty lasted only two weeks, then all the beautiful yellow flowers died. Since the green looked healthy, I cut back the dead, re-potted the roots, added more soil, and watered the pot well. So far, this is my closest attempt at real gardening.

Two of my favorites are a pink mounding Mandevilla I learned about from my daughter and a dusty yellow Aloha Kona Calibrachoa, like one I had last year, but now I know the name. I also bought a larger pot of mixed pink and red geraniums with a pinkish green spiked plant in the center that wasn't named on the label. These flowers were made available from a reputable source for sale in our location, I presume based on their being suited to the climate.

After filling my cart with flowers based on size, color, and condition, but without help or advice, I paid at the checkout. I didn't expect the person at the register to know much beyond being able to accept payment and provide a receipt. I was right. A few days later, I returned and I asked the nearest person wearing an orange Home Depot vest if the marigolds had come in. She said, "I don't know," and relayed my question to another worker. This person responded, "What do they look like?" That's all I needed to know!

At the big-box store you will receive none of the personal attention or special tips available at the typical garden store. If you want this kind of support, it would be best to head there first. For example, you may want to know if the flowers you purchased require pinching back the dead, or how to water and fertilize. In my garden, when it comes to pinching back, this is required for the African daisy and the geranium but not the Mandevilla or Pericallis. That's OK. Doing it makes me feel a bit more like a farmer.

For the minimal effort and modest expense, my garden is an ongoing joy and it would be hard to imagine meeting spring without making this effort.

Next, we'll hear from Bruce, who digs in the dirt, gets his hands dirty, and makes his yard beautiful for all to enjoy.

I ENJOY DIRT

My love of gardening did not totally develop until my wife and I bought our first and only home in 1969, when I was twenty-nine. But I suspect that the genes for gardening had been growing for quite some time. My Scottish ancestors owned a castle, a garden, and were farmers. In 1721, George Hume immigrated to Virginia as an alternative to hanging when his side lost in the first Jacobite Revolution with the English. Pardoned as a bonded servant by then retiring Governor Spotswood, George Hume became a surveyor sponsored by Lord Fairfax. His papers are in the University of Virginia Library. He was also a farmer. For the next two hundred and seventy-nine years or so, the Humes, the Sniders (my grandmother), the Deatons, (my grandmother's family), the Turners (my grandfather's family) either farmed or taught school. One of my great-grandparents was a banker but returned to farming.

Much of the same farming history exists for my wife's German ancestry starting in the 1830s. Playing, planting, and working in the dirt was a way of life.

Fast forward to my mom and dad. They both were teachers and gardeners, but on retirement went back to farming. I not only grew up in the suburbs with flowers and a vegetable garden, but I had to mow and pick vegetables and snap green beans. As I have aged, I have given up vegetable gardening.

My wife and I now concentrate on flowers, shrubs, and trees. Our front garden has a Japanese yew, a full-sized boxwood, three columnar boxwoods, a variegated iris, an ornamental Japanese tree, astilbe, ferns, New York asters, New England asters, potted geraniums, purple and beige cone flowers, moonbeam coreopsis, blue Midnight May salvia, lavender, day lilies, and shasta daisies and a blue spruce bush. Our first Christmas at Marquette we were in a small apartment so we ordered a twenty-one-inch Alberta Spruce tree from L.L. Bean, which became our Christmas tree that year. When we moved to the cottage, Wilson helped us plant that tree in a pot that sits outside by our garage. It is twenty-seven and one-half inches high now. Having Wilson available as an expert is helpful to us.

We also have miniature boxwoods and two evergreen trees on the west side of the cottage. To replace some dead trees, we received a red maple in the front yard, a tulip poplar, a red maple and a dogwood tree in the backyard.

In the backyard we also started a small garden. Currently we have coral bells, shasta daisies, sedge grass, and purple bellflowers. We have Virginia Creeper growing up a trellis against the back of the cottage. Three Japanese yews line the sidewalk. A hanging pot on the fence holds creeping Jenny, alyssum, white euphorbia, and dark-blue lobelia. A potted red geranium sits in a wrought-iron stand.

We planted mostly native Indiana plants with a color theme of yellow, green, and purple—the Mardi Gras colors (that was by accident). Occasionally we use red or white plants for some variety.

It is all fun, as playing in dirt should be.

Balcony Gardening —It Must be 5 O'clock Somewhere

by Jackie King

Congratulations, Jackie, for successfully mastering the Grow Box and for sharing your experience. Now we look forward to a lush garden that was promised you in 70 or so days. I am looking forward especially to the tomatoes.

After 52 years of taking care of a house, yard, and garden, my husband and I decided to move to a retirement community and into an apartment. I had always planted flowers, taken care of bushes, and tried to reach that unattainable goal of having a "no work" perennial garden.

This year is the balcony-gardening trial. After hearing that my brother-in-law was buying grow boxes for his deck, since he and my sister are not able to work their garden, I decided to give it a try. Here is the situation so far.

First, search the Internet for grow boxes, which leads me to all kinds of places to grow marijuana and other associated products. Then, choose a box, yea, they come with wheels too. Order the box and the recommended grow mix—not dirt or soil, mind you, but a specialized product called *grow mix*. Then wait, as the order comes in three separate deliveries over five days. Anxiously opening the boxes, I start reading the directions. First, assemble the box, OK. Then, do something to the grow mix that requires a consultation with my brother-in-law. Two days later, I am set to begin again. Go to step two ,which says spread a specialized soil conditioner into the mix. Another trip to the nursery section. However, I read ahead and also noted that I needed to buy fertilizer. Good work, I'm ahead of the game.

Step four says to mix all the ingredients and then place the mulch cover over the box while snipping places for the planned plants. Who had time to buy plants yet?

OK, plants in place and all mixtures ready, now it is time to really plant. So today is cold and a little windy, but I am an experienced gardener and am up to the job. Ha, balcony gardening has very little room for error and no place to sweep my mistakes or messes off to. Grow mix is light and blows around with the lightest wind, water always spills into the mix making mud pies on the balcony. So now I finally place the tomato plants, kohlrabi, and sugar snap peas into the container and some marigolds just for color in the corner. Get it all done while only breaking one flower bud off and get set for step 10. Water the bottom part of the container through the fill tube as the system wicks water to the mix and plants grow magically. However, one last mess, step 10 says to water until the overflow holes spill out water. More mess for the balcony floor!

Ninety minutes later, two trips into the apartment, remove shoes, get water, return, replace shoes, water and watch the overflow spill all over the floor, sit back and enjoy. That's when I decided it must be 5 o'clock someplace and found the appropriate libation.

I will keep you updated on this effort, or I may just knock on your door with delicious tomatoes in 70 days or so.

100-Year-Old Doll

by Beverly Heid

Treasures, sometimes of high value and others whose main value is sentiment and memories, pass through families over generations. They affect the people involved in very different ways. Here is a heart-warming story that ends just like it should due to the perseverance of one mother.

And the ritual would begin … My mother would gather her four daughters into the bedroom. She would open the closet door to bring out her baby doll.

"This is my baby doll. My grandfather gave me this doll when I was a little girl. I named her Mary Ann."

Then she would say, "You can't play with her." And she would put the doll back into the closet.

I was so taken aback with that selfishness.

I told our two daughters they should share. I would tell them a story about a little girl who would not share her doll. In fact, she hid the doll in a closet. Then I would tell my daughters that her selfishness denied her the doll too. When she went to get her doll out of the closet, the doll's face had melted!

No such thing happened to my mother's baby doll, Mary Ann. She stayed with Mother throughout Mother's adult life. Mother was almost ninety years old when she died.

My older sister, Joan, placed Mary Ann in Mother's casket. Once the evening viewing was over, Joan removed the doll and declared that she was keeping it for herself.

So much for sharing.

Joan collected dolls. When she died, her son and daughter-in-law were involved in the distribution of Joan's belongings. They placed the many collectible dolls, face down, in two rooms in Joan's house. When I entered, all of the dolls had price tags, including Mother's Mary Ann. I was very disappointed and surprised.

I removed Mary Ann from the collection. As we were driving home, my husband informed me that the doll was not mine to take. We turned around. I returned the doll, complete with price tag, to the bedroom.

I sent my nephew and his wife a note offering to pay the price for the doll. I was the only living one of Mother's four daughters. I thought the doll should go to me. I also had two daughters. The other three sisters had only boys.

Their message was that I could take the doll … and give it to our oldest daughter! I had another doll that my sister Joan wanted our daughter to have, so both girls had a family doll.

Our oldest daughter lives in Phoenix. She says I should keep Mary Ann for now. I have put the doll on a chair with a special purple-velvet pillow, hand stamped and made by our daughter Beth Ann. We talk about it once in a while.

I inquired at Riley Hospital about their doll collection case. They said it was a one-time project.

Beth Ann, our daughter, will have to decide Mary Ann's fate.

I would guess that the beautiful doll is 100 years old. Mother was born in 1911. This is 2019. I suppose that Mother received the doll about 1915. The doll has markings from Germany.

All of these years I wished that Mary Ann had been loved by little girls. My baby doll Susie is still with Beth

Ann, although Susie has been repaired more than once. Both of our daughters loved Susie just as much as I did.

Maybe Beth Ann will find a good home for Mary Ann someday.

My Name is Sophie

by Ruth Keenan Hillmer

Pets can be a healthy addition to a senior living community, both for the owners and for other residents who may not be able to manage a pet full-time but enjoy interacting with their neighbors' pets. There are responsibilities when it comes to pets in a senior facility and these are born almost entirely by the human in the equation. Let's hear from one such senior living pet.

Hello! My name is Sophie Hillmer and I am an eight-pound miniature poodle. I live with Marc and Ruth in a cozy apartment on the third floor. Marc and Ruth, who I consider my dad and mom, passed the test for entering the community, but I had to be interviewed separately by Mr. Steve, the head dog. I even have a picture taken on his lap. He is a nice fellow.

Mom told me to be on my best behavior so Mr. Steve would let me come here to live. She said there are almost 500 people here and that I should treat everyone just like I treat my mom and dad. Every chance I had, I tried to show this and I think it worked.

When I met Mr. Steve, I was being very good and sat quietly until I heard him say I could come here to live. Then I just had to give him kisses. He had a furry chin too.

We moved, the three of us, in January, and my bed and toys came along with us. I had never been in an elevator before but I learned to jump over the opening and help push the doors open when we landed. I love being here. All sorts of kind people stop to give me lovin's and I love that in return. When I go out in the morning, I always get a special lovin's from Mr. Rick, the valet, and from Mr. Bill, the bus driver. Miss Dawn and Miss Jane always have good treats at the reception desk. It helps to remind them by wagging my tail. I love the delicious little bites my folks bring me from the dining rooms. No wonder people say you could easily gain the "freshman 15."

I like my walks and have made friends with Sadie, the Scottie; Cora, the Corgi; Sophie, the Dachshund; and Annie, the Havanese. I never heard of that kind before. I'm a little afraid of the Great Dane, but I bark at her just to show I'm not scared.

I promise I will do my best to guard the Manor and keep all the people safe. One day when I was walking by the front door, I accidentally got my leash caught on a light fixture and an evil wicked goose attacked me. He bit my head until it bled and I was really terrified. I had a real "goose egg" on the top of my head. I was smart though and quickly wriggled out of my collar and ran for the front door.

With me gone, that darn goose got Marc, my dad. He said he couldn't believe how strong that bird's wings were. The people here were so concerned that the very next day they put out coyote posters and moved the nests to keep us all safe. I am so glad I live where people care about each other.

Yesterday on my rounds, I investigated something that looked rather odd to me. They told me it was a flower called a white iris and it wasn't supposed to be there. At first I trembled and crept up to it—stretching as far as I could to sniff. It was ok though, but I wanted to be sure it was safe for everybody.

I try to help clean up any popcorn that might have spilled on the floor by the Tavern, just to do my part in helping keep the place clean. I am told that some people are afraid of dogs. I am sure that wouldn't be the case with me if we had the chance to get to know each other. Anyway, I promise I won't ever hurt anybody—I just like being a good girl and loving everybody.

A Traveler's Tales

by Joe Helveston

It was the end of our second week as full-time campers, when I made the call to the RV repair service. We were concerned about the refrigerator not getting cold enough. The serviceman, Bill, came within the hour and started taking panels off and checking wires. Everything looked good and then he asked me if I noticed anything unusual in the coach. I remembered a metal box located in a compartment under the left front of the coach that was warm to the touch and was giving off a strange odor.

After taking the cover plate off the box, he said to cut the electric to the RV. The wires were shorting out and we were very close to having a fire. While Bill was replacing the defective electric panel, I noticed some dark storm clouds coming towards us and the wind picking up. Nancy and I were standing in the living room area of the coach, watching Bill pull away in his truck, when we heard a loud cracking sound. I turned to my left to look out our side window and saw the giant tree that stood next to the camper lying on the ground. It had fallen away from the camper. We both looked at each other. Was this an omen?

Fortunately, we chose to stay the course. Our winter in Florida was problem-free. We were busy visiting our Florida friends and celebrating the various holidays. With spring came the planning for the return trip to Pennsylvania. Nancy makes the reservations for the campgrounds and I check the camper for any possible problems. The trip started the second week of May. We wanted to reach Pennsylvania before Memorial Day. The weather was cool and sunny and the roads were not too busy. I was beginning to feel really good when I noticed a red light flashing on the dashboard panel and the word warning also lit up.

A Pilot gas station was just ahead, so I pulled in and found a parking area. After pulling in, I turned off the engine, climbed out, and headed for the back of the coach. The compartment where the batteries were stored was giving off a strong odor and the door was hot to touch. When I looked in, I could see the front two batteries smoking and bulging out. Our road service rep gave us the name of a local repair service, which we called.

The mechanic, whose name was Mike, asked some questions and told me to take a picture of the batteries and send them to his phone. He was going to stop by his shop on his way to us to pick up replacement batteries. Mike replaced the batteries and then gave us the bad news. He knew what the problem was but he would not be able to fix it himself. We would have to find a local repair shop to do the work. Mike started making phone calls and talking to various service people. It was close to two hours before he finally found one that agreed to do the work. When he gave us his bill, I could see that there was no charge for all his time finding that repair shop. We thanked him for his special efforts and he said he likes to help people.

The repair shop was about twenty miles down the road and we got there about 6:00 PM. The service manager told us we needed an alternator for the engine and he would start trying to locate one. The next day was Friday and Monday was a holiday. If he was unable to get the part by tomorrow, we would be there till Tuesday, which was the day of our grandson's high school graduation in Pennsylvania. The service manager offered to let us stay there overnight and even allowed us to plug in the coach. He personally went and got some ice for us.

He knew we needed to leave Friday to make the graduation. So when he came to the coach the next morning, he had a big smile on his face. He brought news that they had found a part and, if all went well, we could leave that afternoon. When we got the bill I noticed it was much less than the original estimate. I asked why the difference and the lady smiled and said, "The boss gave you a little break!" She then handed us two bags full of coffee cups, note pads, pens, and other great little items. Both Nancy and I felt as we drove down the road that good people and good luck were traveling with us.

Country Morning

by Adrienne Faist

A reflection on the beauty of a country morning celebrates a pristine time that can be a metaphor for life itself.

"Stop! Help!" I hear myself scream, as the automobile ruthlessly bears down upon me. People are striding along the sidewalk just a few long feet from me, but they keep right on about their business. Just as the car is about to strike me down, an irritating jangling noise interrupts near my right. I leave the tragic scene behind with relief, and blindly and automatically grope for the button that stops the reprieving alarm.

I slowly and laboriously open my eyes and look around. The blanket is askew, and my feet are cold from hanging over the edge of the bed. I squint at the bright, early-morning sunlight and remember that I'm to take the tractor and mower out to mow a few rounds of hay before breakfast at eight o'clock. The alarm clock reads five-thirty.

I hop out of bed and skip over to the small rectangle of sunlight on the floor, where it is slightly warmer than the rest of the linoleum. By this time, the goose pimples are in their glory, and the temptation to crawl back into my warm bed is all but overpowering.

I slip into my cold, comfortably battered moccasins and proceed to don my rumpled everyday shorts and summer

43

blouse. The goose pimples are still very much present, and I decide to add an old flannel shirt to my costume—one that can be shed as the July sun climbs higher into the sky. I move to the dresser, and after a glance into the mirror, am comforted by the thought that I probably won't be going anywhere today anyway. The reflection dazedly staring back at me reveals a head of hair with what appears to be almost seventeen cowlicks; some faint, reddish impressions across my cheek, from the creases in the pillowcase; and a pair of dreamy, bedroom eyes—a pillow under each one! It's enough to startle anyone to alertness.

I go downstairs and peel a banana while wondering how anyone could get up any earlier and still survive. I step outside into the cool, fresh, morning air and it seems that the earth is never as clean as in the early morning. The thought occurs to me that this may also be true of life itself—it is never quite so clean as in the very early years.

One of the first sounds to reach my ears is the faint, steady chugging of the milking machine in the barn, and the impatient bawling of a hungry calf. I march down the steps, across the gravel driveway, and into the shadow of the barn, elongated by the sun behind it, and where the grass is still cool and wet, and swishes faintly, seemingly in protest, as my moccasins steal the droplets from it.

I reach the barn, which smells of straw, animals, and warm milk, and hesitate a moment on the doorstep to fondle a kitten or two that comes eagerly running at the sound of my footsteps. I proceed to the rear of the barn, where Dad is milking the placid, ever-cud-chewing cows, and ask him if there are any 'last minute' instructions before I go out to the hayfield behind the barn. He says, "No, I opened the field last night, so you don't have to worry about the outside round. Just be careful on the corner—you may have to loop them, and always watch so the blades don't clog up. I'll let you know when it's time to come in." Thus informed, I make my way back through the barn and outside.

Country Morning

The waiting tractor, with mower hitched to it, is parked under the wide spreading limbs of the aged and friendly box elder tree. I look out across the fields and my eyes take in the misty haze, the silvery green meadows laden with sparkling dew, and a few black-and-white cattle grazing here and there. A very peaceful and contented scene, I reflect.

I clamber up onto the tractor seat, pull the ignition lever, and the power springs into action. I roll out to the end of the driveway, stop to look for oncoming traffic, and finding none, continue out onto the road. I pass by a beautiful, but small, wooded section with a stream winding through it, gurgling merrily. I turn into the field, pull up alongside the standing hay, and stop to let the big, treacherous blade down. This accomplished, I again assume my position on the tractor.

I just sit there a few minutes, watching a robin feeding its young and chirping in a nearby wild cherry tree. Those young birds are in their morning, I contemplate. I glance down and see a gopher scurrying under some limp, fallen hay. A pair of butterflies are already at play, their pale-yellow wings fluttering and hesitating as they alight for a second on a large, sweet clover blossom. All around me is nature at its finest, its cleanest, and most innocent.

A car goes by on the road, its top a white-crystal from the dew yet resting there. Probably someone on their way to work. By now it must be about six-thirty. Time to get started.

But still I linger, soaking up, as it were, the cool vitality of the air and surroundings. "Why," I consider, "can't, or don't people remain as fine and clean as the country morning? Maybe that's why everyone wants to stay young, but hates to get up in the morning, because then they can already see the end of the day approaching. I wonder...."

Well, I'd better get to work now, or Mom will have breakfast ready before I even get started.

Christmas Blessings

by Beverly Heid

"I don't want a tree this year. Our apartment is too small. We've had so much stress in the last year and a half. I am tired. My husband is tired. Let's just forget it."

Those were my words.

Our daughter Sara had a different plan.

Recently, Sara was hospitalized for more than three weeks. One night she almost died, as the liquid around her heart and lungs took her oxygen level down to 52 percent.

God apparently had another plan. Sara recovered. She is back living in our house with her nineteen-year-old son.

What stress I went through as she had her second bout with near death in less than a year. All of this started happening shortly after my two major surgeries (with difficulties) last year.

Surprise!

Sara and friend Amanda put up our Christmas decorations here in our small apartment yesterday.

Sometimes I just don't know what to think about all these stresses … her health problems and mine.

How can I relax? How can I "Let go and let God"?

This morning my husband, Bob, awoke with a cramp in his right leg. I "sprang out of bed" (I was already awake at 5 a.m.) to rub his leg. Now he is back asleep. But I've been up ever since. Here I am, drinking coffee and enjoying all of the Christmas lights and décor in our small apartment.

I've been thanking God for blessings, as I gaze at the Christmas ornaments people have made for us in years past and those we have purchased from prior good times. My dad painted the Santa picture just before he died in 1969. He was so talented. How lucky I've been to have been born into a family with such a loving and talented father.

What about the piano? My husband bought that for me with part of his inheritance from his mother who played the piano.

Whenever I question our moving to such a small apartment, I'm reminded of how many people here at Marquette have appreciated the music gift God gave me.

Today's Bible verse was so fitting and timely.

An email just came announcing my "StoryWorth" book would be delivered today. Hooray! Another blessing. I worked so hard on that book. I'm anxious to share it.

Enough said. It's time to put on my compression garments and eat breakfast. Today, the doctor will be checking the progress made in the last month by wearing those hose and wraps. Can more be done with those leaky valves in my legs?

"Be still before the Lord and wait patiently for him." (Psalm 37:7)

Onward.

Thank God for another day.

Medical Memoir of an Irish Catholic

by Patrick C. Logan

A powerful personal statement kicks off this Chapbook companion to Your Good Life Weekly.

Born in 1935 in a middle-class family in Dayton, Ohio, I was second oldest of eight children. My father was disabled when I was twelve years old. My fourteen-year- older brother, John, and I took over the family appliance-repair business, with the help of our Grandfather Joseph, who had a strong influence on my early years.

During my senior year in high school, I had no plans for college due to lack of money and working to help support our family. I saw an ad for a four-year NROTC scholarship. The Navy required good grades, a written exam, and physical fitness. I chose Notre Dame in 1953. As a strong Catholic, Notre Dame was a dream for me. There I deepened my faith in God, learned to study, and grew up. While I was away at college, my brother John took over the family business. Summers in college were spent taking Navy cruises to Europe plus flight training and amphibious warfare exposure. My major was physics, but it was too narrow for my interest.

After my sophomore year, I visited my Uncle Jerry, a medical student at St. Louis University. He showed me the cadaver lab and when I did not freak out, he encouraged me to switch my studies to pre-med. This was a major turning point in my career. At school it was an honor to work closely with the President of Notre Dame, Father Ted Hesburgh.

He was my mentor and an inspiration to me. While attending my senior year Orientation Weekend, I met the love of my life on a blind date. Sharon was a freshman at nearby St. Mary's College. As Student Body President, I had many extracurricular activities, combined with a demanding pre-med course. I still found time to court Sharon, my future wife of sixty years. We dated steady my entire senior year and on Valentine's Day I gave Sharon a Notre Dame miniature ring, so we were committed to each other.

Graduation weekend was bittersweet. I received my BS in pre-med and was commissioned in the Navy. I left for three years active duty while Sharon finished college. I was assigned as damage control officer on the *USS Camberra*, a guided missile cruiser. Luckily, I was never faced with any ship's fires or battle damage. Our ship visited Turkey and many European ports, and on January 1, 1959, we visited Guantanamo Bay Cuba on the day Fidel Castro became President to the delight of Cuban workers. Little did they know what was coming.

I attended a Navy school and was assigned new duties on the ship: atomic, biological, and chemical warfare officer. After two years at sea, I was assigned to the Maine Maritime Academy to teach Naval history. I immediately called Sharon to set our wedding date. We were married at Notre Dame, in the original log cabin, and a week later moved to Castine, Maine. This was an idyllic seacoast town of 500 souls. Our first son, Patrick, was born nine months after our wedding.

I started Indiana University School of Medicine, and four years later, we had three children. I was able to work part-time so my wife could be a full-time mom. We moved to UCLA for internal medicine internship and moved back to Indiana University for more internal medicine training. At Wishard Hospital, the intern on my service was drafted. I applied for his spot in the dermatology residency. This was the start of a fifty-year fulfilling career in dermatology in East Indianapolis.

Dermatology includes diagnostic challenges as well as surgery. My philosophy of practice is to provide the best medical care to my patients at a reasonable cost. Today, I teach residents and students in my office and at Indiana University Medical School and have felt honored when several of them chose to become dermatologists. Teaching has kept me enthused about medicine. I learn as much from students as they learn from me.

All my office employees have become long-term associates. My third set of office staff have worked with me about fifteen years and are like family. I am still practicing medicine (until I get it right) and enjoy treating many long-time patients. In 2001, I was honored to receive The Doctor of the Year Award given by *Indiana Business Journal*. In 2010 I won the Hackney-Norins award as top dermatologist in Indiana and in 2017 was honored by the American Academy of Dermatology as volunteer of the year for work in Honduras

A few pearls to my readers: Have a total body skin exam annually after age fifty to rule out skin cancer and melanoma; avoid sunburns and tanning beds; use sunscreen SPF 50 in the sun; and take good care of your largest organ, your skin.

Fire and Ice—
Iceland

by Rosemary Hume

Pingvellir National Park. This national park in Iceland is where the Althing, an open-air assembly representing the whole of Iceland, was established in 930 A.D. It continued to meet until 1798

What do Pingvellir National Park, Halldór Laxness, Vigdis Finnbogadottir, Seljalandsfoss, Parfasti Pjonninn, E-15, Strokkur, and the Aurora Borealis, have in common? They are all geographically or historically connected to Iceland.

Iceland is a European country the size of our Pennsylvania. Iceland became a free democratic country in 1944, while Denmark was being invaded by the Nazis.

Mr. Laxness won the Nobel Prize in Literature in 1955 writing *The Independent People. Atlantic Monthly* said this about his work: "A strange story, vibrant and alive ... There is a rare beauty in its telling, a beauty as surprising as the authentic strain of poetry that lies in the shoving, battering Icelander." When one visits Iceland, one wants to know more about its history and its people. Mr. Laxness's book introduces you to this land and its people.

E15 is the name of the place where the 2010 volcano spewed so much ash from its cauldron that international flights had to be canceled for lack of visibility over Iceland. The name of this volcano site in southern Iceland was so difficult for the journalists to pronounce that they nick-named it the E15 site. Its name is Eyjafjallajokull. The researchers found that this volcano violently reacted with nearby glacial water. This rapid cooling made the magma contract and fragment into fine, jagged motes of ash. Near the end of the eruption, equally fine, porous ash was gen-erated when small gas bubbles trapped in the molten rock expanded as the magma neared the surface. This volcanic activity had the effect on the atmosphere causing the air-lines to cancel flights.

Vigdis Finnbogadottir became the world's first demo-cratically directly elected female president in the world. Her political campaigns encouraged reforestation of Iceland. She served from 1980 to 1996. Iceland is slowly planting trees, mostly birch and aspen, which provide a beautiful fall golden landscape next to the lava, mountains, green grasses, and mosses. She likens cultivating trees to bring-ing up children, saying that cultivating the land had close connections to nurturing humans. That cultivation has its foundation in how young people are raised. Vigdis contin-ues to serve as a UNESCO Goodwill ambassador.

Seljalandsfoss is one of 10,000 waterfalls of Iceland. It is connected to the Seljalands River and has its origin in the volcano glacier Eyjafjallajokull. The interesting part of this waterfall is that you can walk behind the waterfall and on trails that go to the top and to other waterfalls.

Parfasti Pjonninn (most useful servant) are the famous Icelandic horses. They are unusual compared to European horses. They were introduced to Iceland by the first Nordic settlers. They have adapted to the cool climate by growing a thick overcoat for winter, which they shed in the spring. They are known as useful servants since they provide trans-portation for the residents when the roads are bad. These horses have unusual additional steps in addition to the conventional walk. These steps are the *tolt* or running walk and the *skeio* or flying pace. Because the horse has these steps, they can provide a comfortable ride in the saddle. Icelandic horses are special to the Icelandic people.

Strokkur provides wonderful scenery. The eruption pours forth from the earth a geyser that starts as a blue bubble. Iceland is on a hot spot. Iceland rests on the boundary where the North American and Eurasian tectonic plates meet. It is also an area of intense volcanic activity and geothermal energy. The blue bubble erupts about every ten minutes.

The Aurora Borealis, or Northern Lights, pulse across the winter sky. The lights originate in the sun as charged particles that move from the sun and contact with the earth's magnetic field and ultimately drawn to the magnetic poles. You need to choose a cold, clear, moonless night around 11 p.m. or 3 a.m. You can download an aurora forecast app to check for times and forecasts.

To experience awe, we suggest visiting Iceland through books, videos, or photos. We want to return.

Hospice

by Margaret Hall Simpson, RN, BSN

Dying is the biggest event in one's life. A person, aware of their imminent death, must be afforded the opportunity to do this with dignity.

Hospice is a concept ... not a place. The care of a terminally ill person may take place anywhere a nurse, trained in the Hospice Philosophy, is available. Care of a terminally ill patient differs drastically from the care of a patient who is expected to be cured or rehabilitated or an elderly, long-term care patient.

The term "palliative care" is sometimes used in the United States to designate a regimen of care with the goal of keeping the terminally ill patient as pain-free as possible while allowing them to be alert and aware. Hospice care is more. A hospice nurse is trained, not only in the care of a person who is dying, but in the support of the family and extended family.

In addition to excellent bedside care, a hospice nurse is sensitive to the phases the patient is experiencing and is there to listen while assessing pain level and monitoring medication. A dying patient should not be expected to turn on a nurse call light and rate their pain on a scale of one to ten in order to be properly medicated, nor have to wait until the next dose is due four hours later. Medication must be given before pain returns, not after the pain has escalated.

A dying patient should not be urged to eat or drink. They will not die of starvation. They will die of their disease process. It is a normal response by the family to want to try to get the patient to take food; however, it could only cause additional stress for the patient. Keeping the mouth, tongue, and lips clean and moist with swabs is essential. Simply putting water in a patient's mouth may allow the fluid to enter the lungs. The patient will not die of dehydration. In fact, dehydration is a natural form of anesthesia.

Bowel and bladder functions may be a source of severe discomfort. Narcotics may cause constipation. The hospice nurse will be aware of the patient's bodily functions and remedy the situation before it causes additional pain. Frequently, decubitus ulcers (bedsores) caused by pressure on bony prominences occur when a patient has been on bedrest for an extended time. Poor diet lacking sufficient protein contributes to skin breakdown. Relieving the pressure by turning and repositioning every two hours, keeping the areas clean and dry, and gentle massage helps prevent decubitus ulcers. After they appear, it is very difficult to cure them.

Dying is the greatest event in one's life. A person, aware of their imminent death, must be given the opportunity to talk about death. It is understandable that this is difficult for a family. They may say, "Let's not talk about that now. You'll feel better tomorrow." Refusing to listen to the patient diminishes the importance of their death. Listening to what the person is experiencing emotionally, without judging or interrupting, is an important duty of a hospice nurse.

When the patient reaches the stage of actively dying, family members at the bedside may notice the extremities are becoming cold and may appear bluish and "mottled."

In their desire to "hold on" to the loved one, or delay the moment of death, they may want to massage the legs and hands. Not only does this not, in any way, delay death, it is disturbing to the patient. Those at the bedside should, gently, be made aware that this is not helpful.

It may also be beneficial to instruct those at the bedside to refrain from requesting the patient to do anything that would require a response or action, such as: "Squeeze my hand if you can hear me" or "blink your eyes." The dying patient is preparing emotionally and should be allowed a quiet and peaceful time without external stimuli. It is believed that hearing is the last of the senses to leave the human body. Discussing funeral arrangements or dividing assets should take place elsewhere. Talking softly at the bedside may be comforting to the patient and catharsis for the family.

A patient may be clinging to life, feeling they are abandoning their loved ones, and need "permission" to "let go." Hospice nurses are sensitive to grief, not only the grief of those at the bedside, but the grief the patient is experiencing, grief for the life they are losing.

Hospice will do nothing to extend life, neither will hospice do anything to shorten life.

While Dad Went to War

by Sandra Hamilton

A heartwarming story of a little girl's time in a safe, idyllic setting while her dad served in the Navy.

My children, for a good part of their formative years, were raised in a beautiful neighborhood on Washington Boulevard in Indianapolis. Like my grandchildren now, their "free time" was scheduled with school activities, sports, and social commitments like lines on a dance card. Recently I reflected on a time in my early childhood when social activities were not so organized and nearby neighbors were nonexistent.

We lived, at the time, in Mt. Vernon, a small city in Westchester County, New York. I had just started kindergarten when my dad enlisted in the Navy in 1942. Mom was less than happy when he announced this, since he was thirty-two, already a government employee, and had an exemption. But Uncle Sam said yes; he was off on a ship in the Atlantic in a very short time.

My brother, two years older; myself; and Mom moved to live in Suffern, New York. An army-olive-green sedan, driven by a uniformed Red Cross lady, drove us there, since I had the measles. I felt a certain degree of importance to be conveyed in such a way as we headed to country living.

57

Suffern was a very rural area then, and we settled into a small cottage rental on Mr. and Mrs. Barnhart's property of many acres. Bruno, a middle-aged farmhand, kept the landscaped grounds surrounding us, tended the 100 chickens brought in each spring, and tilled several acres with a horse-pulled plough for the potatoes, beans, peas, and tomatoes planted for our use and the Barnhart's throughout the year.

Watching Bruno tend to his many chores fascinated me. Our home was the rustic guest cottage. There was one pot-bellied stove for heat, and many a winter's night Mom would put a towel-wrapped warm brick between our bed sheets for warmth. The trick was to fall asleep before it cooled off.

Though isolated, for me it was an enchanting time. I loved the country, the woods surrounding our property, the delightful trickling stream that rippled so gently through it, which birthed polliwogs that miraculously turned into frogs every spring. We named the sand bar in it "Solomon Island." I can still hear those fluffy yellow chicks, purchased each spring, chirping under the warming lights in the basement. I was horrified months later when Bruno decapitated one or two hens for our dinner.

The big barn that housed winter hay and all sorts of tools certainly was the BEST playhouse ever provided two children. Mom never caught us when we built giant hay mounds to jump into from the loft ten feet above. It was hide-and-seek heaven, a pirate's harbor, and a fort to ward off attacking Indians!

When fall came, my brother, Jim, and I walked half a mile to catch the school bus. On the way, we might pass deer herds, who came out of the woods to forage for breakfast in the open fields. Their heads would snap to attention and stare us down while assessing the degree of danger we presented. Ours was literally a little red school house of four rooms for eight grades. Each room had two grades in it, and somehow young, lovely Miss Crumb kept the twelve or so students in each grade busied with instruction on one side of the room, while the other half did paper work. It was delightful, interesting, and always orderly.

Saturdays were special. Bruno drove us into the small town of Suffern. We'd go to a matinee. My first movie was the never to be forgotten *Bambi*, followed by an ice cream cone … surely manna from heaven. Mom would carefully count her ration stamps to see if we had enough for a roast at the butcher shop or maybe some real butter or for a pair of new shoes. It seemed that everything was rationed. I remember asking my mother what did they put in the newspaper when there was no war. Returning to our cottage, the three of us would huddle around our radio, wrapped in blankets to tune in Kate Smith, who always ended the show singing "God Bless America."

The best of all memories was an annual greyhound bus trip to Ringling Brother's Barnum and Baily Circus at Madison Square Garden. Dinner followed at the Automat. While the man painted on the huge billboard above Broadway puffed his perfect, gigantic circles of smoke, we could choose whatever we wanted from walls of glass and stainless steel compartments serving individual portions of all kinds of food for our dinner. Just drop in your quarters and out the food came. No rationing stamps needed! There was Magic to me in the big city.

In the spring of my second grade, I tearfully approached Miss Crumb and said I had something to tell her. As I sat on her lap at the teacher's desk, I gave her the news that Dad was coming home from the War and we had to move back to Westchester. Little did I know that she knew my father had been discharged to be with us. Mom had cancer, and following a double mastectomy, she died the following year in the bedroom of our new home. It was the house which my grandfather built in the early 1900s. It was in the small town of Eastchester, ten miles north on Route 22 from our first home in Mt. Vernon.

Looking back, I believe the independence of country living helped me adjust well to the new, different life of growing up, which lay ahead.

9/11 Mexico City Flight Diverted

by Marion Harcourt

Recollections of a Red Cross Mental Health Volunteer

After the attacks on September 11, 2001, the FAA ordered all planes in the air to land immediately. This included a flight of Mexican businessmen and their wives who had attended a conference in Toronto and were on their way home to Mexico City. Their plane landed in Indianapolis, and they were stranded.

The airport notified the Red Cross, whose charge is to respond immediately to care for stranded people, whether from a tornado, an apartment fire, a hurricane, or anything they so designate. In this case, it was an airport "disaster" but on a personal scale.

The Red Cross arranged for the use of Jameson Camp near Bridgeport, not far from the airport, to host the visitors. The facility provided beds, lavatories, and dining facilities for the two hundred or so guests.

The Red Cross then put out a call for their trained volunteers to come to the site to care for the stranded travelers. The police made the camp a secure area. Allowing the public to enter was not safe as there was no way to screen visitors. This was not Gander Newfoundland, a celebrated port of entry in Canada that was lauded for its unique out-pouring of hospitality.

The stranded passengers had Mexican passports and no Visas for legal entry into the U.S. They could not leave the camp. The Red Cross arranged for local restaurants to donate food. "Thank you, McDonald's, among others." With this help, the Red Cross volunteers set up a dining area.

Wishard Hospital established a temporary emergency clinic to respond to any acute medical needs. The Red Cross has authority for its healthcare workers to validate and fill prescriptions in an emergency. The Red Cross mental health team responded to issues, especially helping to deal with the stress brought on by the events. That was my job. Other workers retrieved luggage from the plane and drove travelers to a laundry.

After the second day, life got BORING! Our group brought playing cards, board games, and stationery to give our guests something to occupy their time. We also brought in several televisions, some equipped for Spanish speakers, so they could keep abreast of the news in the days following 9/11. We arranged for phone stations, necessary because cell phones were not widely available. These were equipped to allow calls to Mexico.

Finally, we received permission from Immigration allowing people to leave the property for brief periods. I was selected to be the docent from Indiana Landmarks to conduct tours of the city, including Monument Circle, The Capital, Indianapolis Motor Speedway, Eagle Creek, and the grounds of the Indianapolis Museum of Art.

Most of the men spoke English but some of the wives didn't. There were plenty of Spanish-speaking Red Cross volunteers and that helped.

It was nearly a week before air traffic resumed fully. Officials countrywide had an enormous job untangling the mess caused by the necessary departures and arrivals. Finally, the Mexican guests were on their way home.

Indianapolis was not equipped to welcome our guests in the celebrated way it happened with our Canadian neighbors, but our guests were well taken care of and seemed to enjoy their brief unplanned stay in central Indiana.

My Role in the U.S. Air Force

by Bruce Hume

I was a project engineer and the sky was the limit.

In July 1963, after graduation from The Ohio State University, I was posted to Vandenberg Air Force Base in Lompoc, California. There I remained until January 1966.

Between the graduation at The Ohio State University and Vandenberg AFB, I did approximately five weeks in AT&T's Long Lines Management Training Program. That company hired me knowing about my service obligation. My five-year university degree was for a B. S. in Industrial Engineering. In reality, it was more of a degree in Project Management.

My assignment at Vandenberg AFB was to the 6595th Aerospace Test Wing, specifically the Atlas-Agena Project Office. The Atlas-Agena was a booster/satellite program designed to put a General Electric payload into north-south orbit around the earth. The north-south orbit from Vandenberg AFB allowed the U.S. to launch over water in case of having to abort the launch. The payload allowed the United States to take pictures of our adversaries.

The project office job was to represent the Air Force in terms of accepting the Atlas booster and other stages of the launch package from the various other suppliers that made those stages of the satellite. For example, Kodak made the camera that was used as the payload. The project office was responsible for the approval of the electrical and mechanical assemblies and tests that were done at the factory.

After the stages were sent to Vandenberg, the project office approved and helped the suppliers replicate the tests that were run back at the factory. The project office then shipped the entire launch vehicle to the launchpad where the booster vehicle and stages were tested again.

While vertical, the various stages of the assembly were fueled and launched. When the flight was completed the nosecone with the film was ejected, a parachute was opened, and the nosecone and the film was retrieved by an airplane. The airplane hooked the rigging of the parachute as it came down and before it landed in the ocean.

During my almost three years in the Atlas-Agena Project Office, I received the equivalent of a master's degree in Project Management. This became the center of my civilian career after I left the military. I will be forever grateful to the U.S. Air Force and the Department of Defense Contractors with whom I worked. I was proud to have received that assignment and I was proud of the job that our office did.

To my "Spy in the Sky" friends and to Humphrey Bogart, "Here's looking at you, babe."

Scatting

by Rosemary Hume

An interesting take on a singing style popular with entertainers in our youth, which we rediscovered in the senior years.

As Brenda Williams sings and then scats at the jazz performance at our retirement center, I become interested in the scatting approach she is taking during the time that the piano player and bass player played their solo jazz accompaniment to her performance. I think that the microphone is not working appropriately. She adjusts the microphone but what I hear is "gibberjabber."

After talking with other residents, they helped me remember the name of gibberjabber that singers use. People like Ella Fitzgerald tried to imitate sounds of other instruments by singing, or scatting, melodies. She used her voice as an instrument rather than a speaking or singing voice.

Scat singing can give jazz singers the same opportunity as jazz instrumentalists have, the ability to improvise. Some say, "Scat don't mean anything but just something to give a song a flavor." Scat singing says random words or phrases that are nonsensical while the singer joins the bass player and the piano player as they improvise with the piano and bass. They seem to have fun with it.

Scatting

To learn to scat, you need to practice rhythmic syllables while focusing on a melody. Here are some syllables to practice:

"doo bah doo bah do"
"da bop da bah da"

While you scat, think and act like you are a horn player or a saxophone player and stay in melody. Louis Armstrong is thought to be the first who "scatted"—"Ooh bop sha bam"—when his music fell to the floor and he didn't know the words. But he knew the melody. There were others before Armstrong who scatted; but Louis Armstrong popularized scatting.

In a book titled *Scat*, Bob Stoloff shares a collection of patterns and syllables for use in scatting. His book gives a comprehensive approach to rhythmic and melodic exercises, response exercises, and more. Remember Alvin and the Chipmunks? They employed humorous scatting in their nonsensical syllables—"oo ee oo ah ah."

Scat singing can give jazz singers the same opportunity as jazz instrumentalists. Some say the scat singing "can describe matters beyond words. A great scat performance is able to bypass our ears and our brains and go directly to the heart and soul."*

Other words that are used or are compared to scatting are: gobbleygook, mumbo jumbo, word salad, babbling, and gibberish.

I'd like to go back again to the jazz performance last week and try to listen to the scatting that joined the jazz bass player and piano player. Maybe I will try YouTube.

*Gabbard, Krin. *Representing Jazz*. 1995

The Kellogg "Scholar"

by Gene Helveston

Something small can make a big difference

In the fall of 1957, I was in a pickle. Because of summer school, I had limited time to work. This left me with only $1,000 and I owed all of it for last year's student loan. But I had a plan. I would pay my debt and a week later re-apply. Getting $1,500 with the new loan would take care of tuition and go a long way toward living expenses because I had a very cheap room and a meal job.

With a clean record, I approached the student loan office with confidence. I had repaid my loan on time. I knew a lot of people were having trouble because summer jobs had been hard to get. I should be at the head of the line for acceptance. I approached the clerk seated at a desk and asked for a student loan application. Then it hit!

"I am sorry. We aren't taking any new student loan applications at this time." The young lady maintained a neutral gaze.

I blurted, "Why?"

Matter-of-factly she said, "We have had so many failures of re-payment for last year's loans that we have no funds. You can come back next semester and by that time new loans could be available."

The Kellogg "Scholar"

Only half seriously, I said, "OK, then. Can I have my money back and be like the rest of them?"

With this, the young woman looked up, said no with her head, and that was it. The conversation was over.

Now, for plan two. Since I was never asked if I had paid tuition, I decided to attend classes and figure out how to get the money later. Tuition for medical school was only $275 and I should be able to come up with that some way. I told no one. As the days passed, my sense of urgency diminished but a healthy concern remained. Then, it happened.

I was called to the office of the Academic Dean. I knew he was a retired Methodist minister and a classmate's father-in-law. This would be the first time I met him.

He greeted me cordially and said, "I understand you have been attending classes but have not paid your tuition."

"Yes, sir," I said, and then shared my plight.

His face clouded with concern and he said, "I'm sorry, but you must pay tuition or you will not be able to continue attending classes. I am not in a position to make any exceptions, but I do have sympathy."

"Will I be kicked out now?" I asked.

"No," he said.

"Thank you. I will do my best," I said and left.

Two weeks later, I received a letter from the W.K. Kellogg Foundation. It said: "Congratulations on being a Kellogg Scholar." Enclosed was a check for $375. I had not applied for this and my academic record at the time was not that good.

"Why this money?" I asked myself. It had to be the Dean acting immediately to accomplish this in two weeks.

I paid my tuition and had $100 left. A month later, I received the loan that had been denied and all was well.

This compassionate act by a person I met only once, and for not more than five minutes, was one of the finest gifts I have ever received—a life-shaping event.

Hiking

by Jackie King

A love of hiking and appreciation for how it can benefit a person's life is clearly stated.

"Happiness is one step at a time." This statement is on many of the patches and other materials that publicize the Indianapolis Hiking Club. One of the largest and oldest hiking clubs in the country, there are more than 500 members who hike 1 to 20 times per month. (www.indyhike.org)

I was invited to join the club shortly after moving to Indianapolis and have been happy with that decision. Hiking in the Indy Hike Club is an open definition, hikes take place in the forest where hikers are clad in boots, coats, and hiking sticks; or hikes take place in a mall where we hang our coats up and just wear our sturdy comfy tennis shoes. The long hikes take place on weekends where the trek can be 10–12 miles and last up to 4–6 hours depending on terrain. Most other hikes take place any day of the week and are 3–7 miles long, lasting 2–3 hours. Being somewhat fit is necessary for hiking, but it is surprising how easy it is to just keep taking one step at a time and complete 4–5 miles buoyed by friendly hikers who do not leave anyone behind.

Hiking

In 2016, the centennial for Indiana State Parks, the club decided to challenge its members by scheduling a hike in every state park that year. The inaugural hike was at White River State Park in downtown Indy on January 1. It was a cold day, but 143 people showed up for that hike. By the end of the year, 38 hikers made it to all 25 state parks for a hike! Many others hiked several of the parks. I managed just 5 parks, but most were in new places for me.

What I like about hiking. First it was the sense of accomplishment. After my first 5-mile hike in Eagle Creek Park, I limped to my car, limped to my home, showered, and then just 'rested' for several hours. After becoming more fit, that same hike was just 'a walk in the woods' with none of the aches, pains, and complaining and resting that happened during the first hikes.

Second, the Indianapolis Hiking Club members are some of the most interesting, friendly, and kind people who live here. There is no competition between members; you compete with yourself for mileage and accomplishments.

Third, there is no fashion requirement, meaning hikers wear clothes comfortable for the weather and walking, if you wear the same coat all winter, so be it; if you don't have one article of clothing that was purchased in a hiking section of any store, that's OK.

We hike for exercise and companionship and for the badges. The club provides a name badge with miles achieved at certain intervals. Some members have hiked in excess of 20,000 miles. For me, I have a treasured 2,000-mile achievement badge.

Members volunteer to be hike leaders; some have led the same hike for many years, others volunteer to lead when it's a special occasion, such as "join xxxx for her 70th birthday" hike. Others will create special out-of-town trips and lead hikes there. For 23 years the club has gone to the Smoky Mountains for a long weekend hike in April.

Leaders there vary but there is always someone willing to serve.

In 2014, I organized and led a 6-day hike along Hadrian's Wall in northern England (the average age of 22 hikers was 68 years). Others have hiked in Germany, Switzerland, and recently several more trips to England. Hikes have taken place in northern Michigan, Ohio, California, Illinois, Florida, Virginia, and West Virginia. We even had a Washington D.C. hike led by members who formerly lived and worked in the area. Most of those hikes were 4 to 7 days, with members finding their own way to the starting hike. Still popular are the several times a year when the club hikes on a weekend in Indiana State Parks.

Hiking is one of those activities that gives me a thrill. I am energized after a hike and grateful for being able to be outside whether it's on sidewalks or trails. There is so much that one can see when on foot, even in familiar neighborhoods. The social aspect of hiking with others is important. While members are from very different backgrounds the love of outdoors and nature binds us to each other while hiking.

Find Your Voice

by Carol Weaver

Residents living in a retirement community can find a voice through representation and a receptive administration. This is the experience of one such voice.

As a member of our Resident Council for the past year, I have been able to serve in a very specific and engaging way. I serve as the representative of one of the seven living units in a large urban retirement community.

Our Council is composed of one member each representing five floors in the main buildings, twenty-eight cottages, and forty-four units in an adjoining building. The Council is led by an elected president and vice president. The executive director and his assistant represent management. We meet once a month with additional quarterly meetings with the Executive Committee of the Board of Directors of the institution.

My term of service as a representative is for two years beginning in February. Members serve on a rotating basis with about half of the members going off the Council every year at the end of January and new members coming on to fill these positions. Currently our council members are nominated/appointed from independent living.

The duties of a council member are contained in the

By-Laws of the Council. This article will focus on how I view my role as a member of the Council.

In agreeing to accept the position, I felt that my primary reason for serving was to provide a voice for the residents I would be representing. I would speak with the management on behalf of the more than fifty people who call our part of the community home. When a resident contacts me, it is usually because there has been an issue affecting them that had not been resolved satisfactorily. I have heard these issues described as seeming to have fallen into a "black hole." This is very frustrating to residents as they see little recourse in getting their issues resolved in a timely manner or resolved at all! Other issues deal with new ideas.

After getting my feet wet as a new Council member, I focused my attention on capturing the specific issues of those I represent and began presenting some of them at the regular Council meetings. Others could be resolved outside the meeting by working with management, security, plant services, etc. for discussion and resolution.

Although not always successful, this process did work for me most of the time; many issues were resolved. Targeted approach is the best way I have found to seek and secure resolution of issues for the residents.

To close the loop of communication, I re-contact the resident submitting the issue and let them know the status, such as the date of discussion at the Council meeting, possible solutions, time frame for resolution, and whether or not it can be resolved and reasons why. When a resident's issue could be of general interest/concern I share them with the other members of the Council.

To keep the residents up to date, I put out a resident bulletin every six to eight weeks with a brief discussion of the major issues and their resolution (or planned time frame for solution), as well as general information that may be of interest. I've taken a cue from other Council members and occasionally organize an event, such as a speaker of interest for the residents.

I served as the Resident Association and Resident Council secretary for a year, during which I was responsible for editing and proofreading the minutes of the two meetings each month and filing copies of the finalized versions of each in the library and posting copies. It was a pleasure working with the CEO's assistant each month to ensure the minutes from both meetings were accurate and complete.

Along with the secretary's position came the responsibility to contact and secure two hostesses for the Resident's Association meetings. Many wonderful residents volunteered to help by greeting residents as they entered the meeting room and helping serve food and drinks at the table at the back of the hall. The hostesses rotated each month.

For me, it has been an interesting experience! I have served as I interpret the role of a Council member. Some of my colleagues approach their roles a little differently, but we are all there to represent our respective areas to the best of our abilities.

Thumbs Up to American Airlines

by Ed Koskie

An upbeat story about air travel.

Recent studies of customer satisfaction with airlines have placed American at the bottom of U.S. carriers. My wife and I recently made a round trip to Yuma, Arizona, via American Airlines with a connection in Phoenix. The following is our personal experience.

We were scheduled to leave Indianapolis at 7:50 am (actual departure 7:48 am). On the Phoenix leg, we were served a very nice breakfast of a hot omelet, fruit cup, croissant, yogurt, juice, and coffee. The flight was smooth and pleasurable.

Now, the story has an unusual twist. We arrived in Phoenix slightly early, but to our chagrin, an hour delay for the next leg was posted. The reason was astounding—the airport at Yuma was closed because of a rare event: heavy rain! Yuma advertises 308 days of sunshine per year and average February rain of 0.3 inches!

When we finally took off from Phoenix and arrived near Yuma, the runway was still obscured. We circled for about 25 minutes before the rain finally abated so a safe landing could be made.

Many parking lots in Yuma had at least several inches

of standing water! My sister, who was meeting us, arrived looking like a drowned rat from being caught in the rain between her car and shelter.

Except for Mother Nature's historic "welcome," the flights themselves were excellent. My bag was the second off the plane and my wife's appeared shortly thereafter. Absolutely no problem with American then. Our flight was smooth and safe, the attendants were pleasant and attentive to all our needs. I would give AA an A or, better yet, an AA plus!

On our return from Yuma, we departed a couple of minutes early as everyone was on board and the flight was smooth. Our two-hour layover at Phoenix was as scheduled. We boarded on time and were offered a drink while we waited during boarding. Again, we left a few minutes prior to posted time since everyone was on board. The pilot introduced himself and hoped that this flight would be one of our most pleasurable. The flight was mildly bumpy over the Rockies but, before it started, he advised us that he had asked for a smoother altitude from flight control, but none was available.

The attendant was very conscientious and friendly. She served us wine as soon as the takeoff stabilized and then the meals we had requested as soon as the bumps were over. She was attentive to our every wish for the entire flight.

There was a slight mechanical problem with my tray being very difficult to open, which I reported. At the end of the trip, our flight attendant advised me that she had added 1,000 miles to my frequent flyer account because I reported and tried to fix it!

The wait for bags in Indianapolis was a bit lengthy but still acceptable. And our return trip rated another AA plus for all services provided.

As a final note, I should say that my wife and I had decided to give each other early birthday (hers in March and mine in April) presents of flying first class. Perhaps the flight in coach may not have been quite so pleasant, but for us, our choice was well worth it, and we could not ask for more from American Airlines!

Thank you, American Airlines!

Is It Canceled?
A New Way of Life

by Rosemary Hume

The current crisis finds people working in creative ways.

Besides all the wonderful support the Marquette staff is providing to the residents, I have learned about an interesting approach that was used when Rolling Meadows High School had to cancel their *West Side Story* choir performance. The choir performance had been planned for weeks and the students had practiced for weeks. The students were quite upset, especially the seniors who are anticipating that other end-of-the-year activities will be canceled.

One student crafted an approach using editing apps and had each music student send him a video of their singing their part in the song "Somewhere." He combined all the videos to make a collage of each student in their own home singing the *West Side Story* song "Somewhere." He then put this on Facebook, so we can all see and hear it.

There's a place for us,
Somewhere a place for us.
Peace and quiet and open air
Wait for us
Somewhere.

There's a time for us,
Some day a time for us,
Time together with time to spare,
Time to learn, time to care,
Some day!
Somewhere.
We'll find a new way of living,
We'll find a way of forgiving
Somewhere…
There's a place for us,
A time and a place for us.
Hold my hand and we're halfway there.
Hold my hand and I'll take you there
Somehow,
Some day,
Somewhere!

Thanks to the Rolling Meadows Choir for making our day a special one. They are planning to contribute more songs soon.

If anyone else hears of wonderful ways that people are coping with the reality of today, let us know. We'd love to hear the stories.

Reflections

by Bob Waeltz

Little things can mean a lot.

The recent change to daylight savings time triggered a fond memory. ... After World War II ended, I returned to St. Louis, Missouri, and resumed my studies at Washington University. The school was crowded with veterans on the G.I. Bill, requiring many popular classes to be held in the large auditorium.

On this day there was a test in world history. JoAnne Cates was sitting next to her twin sister, Jeanne, in the balcony. She asked Jeanne, "What time is it?"

The proctor intervened and the next day JoAnne was moved from the balcony down to the main floor in the first row and next to me. She was very attractive, but I was cautioned by the guy she was dating.

Later that summer, I went downtown to Boyd's Department store. There was a large picture of JoAnne in the window. She was called a fashion consultant and model. I decided to give her a call but didn't expect her to say yes when I asked for a date. Fortunately, she accepted the invitation—and the rest is history, as we recently celebrated our 70th wedding anniversary.

The question, "What time is it?" remains a fond memory.

A Liberal Political Refugee

by Federico Dies

A liberal 4-year-old political refugee? Or a pondering 84-year-old adult?

My father, Haroldo Díes, was a Spanish-born official assigned to the French office of the Spanish National Ministry of Tourism. My father and my mother, Pilar Angulo, moved from Madrid to Paris in December of 1935 when he assumed that post. I was traveling incognito in my mother's womb as I was conceived in Spain, but born in Paris in March of 1936.

On July 18, 1936, a group within the Spanish military initiated an attack against the legitimate republican government that had been elected democratically in Spain on April 14, 1931, following the deposition of King Alfonso XIII, thus starting the Spanish Civil War.

My parents were politically liberal: they voted for the Second Republic and against the monarchy in Spain, and they actively opposed the military coup. The Spanish Civil War ended with the victory of General Francisco Franco and his allies in April of 1939.

My parents would not have been allowed to return to live in Spain, at least not freely. So, they stayed in France for a few months until they could board a ship that took them and me to México. We were welcomed as Spanish political refugees thanks to the generosity and foresight of Mexican President General Lázaro Cárdenas. We have been forever grateful. I guess I didn't know it at the time, but at the tender age of almost 4, in January of 1940, I was already a liberal and a political refugee!

I grew up in México in my parent's home. Most of the family friends, almost all, were liberal Spaniard refugees like us. I became, or remained, a political and social liberal with considerable animosity against Franco's regime and, by extension, all other fascist political groups or parties in the world. However, I wonder how many degrees of freedom does one have in order to evolve as an independent thinker? Is the imprint of our early years from family, friends, and school so strong that it determines how and who we are as adults?

In my family, I have what may be as close as one can get to a controlled test. I have two brothers who are identical twins. They grew up in the same environment I did, yet their adult personalities are quite different from each other and from me. From a political perspective, one of them is a centrist, leaning conservative, and the other is a leftist liberal. Politically speaking, one of them is to my right and the other one to my left.

I am almost sure that the right answer to my question is, as is the case almost always, that both early development and life experience play roles in how we come out in the end. This has been the case for me and my brothers. Also, we all know of people whose political, social, and economic views evolve with age and circumstances during their lives.

This is my story. How about yours? Or, as Barbara Furlow would say, "What do YOU think?"

Is it Right?

by Lucy Riegel

Two points connected with a continuous band constitutes a line. The line can be a continuous curve, a parabola, or straight.

We inhabit a right-angle world of constructions. In my apartment, every room is limited by right-angle corners. I inhabit a small rectangular section of the fifth floor of a rectangular building—square corners.

The non-right-angle parts of the building appear to be more decorative than functional. Their purpose is to highlight the right angles that dominate. Example: the curved roofs of the entry canopies are there to beautify the entrance. The curved wall of the swimming pool adds interest, but it inhibits lap swimming which is always carried out at right angles from the end of the pool. This morning, as I participated in a water aerobics class, I noticed each group of four participants were aligned in a square formation, or were they equidistant points in a circle?

A visit to Google seeking insight yielded little. Right angles are not usual in nature. A tree which rises perpendicular from its base in the ground, forming a right angle is an exception. And some natural quartzite breaks along

straight lines. There is also some esoterica dealing with this
—metaphysical musings?

We think of space all around us—yet there are four
cardinal directions determined by man who designed them
to intersect at right angles. Ditto for clocks—literature
focuses on time in the half—hour, the quarter, and noon
straight up. (Of course, such distinctions may be lost as we
go to abbreviations for direction on GPS and digital time.)

Visit ancient ruins like Ephesus, Aztec remnants,
Chinese soldiers, Machu Picchu. Much of the construc-
tion is on right angles. Not the coliseum or the Pantheon
though. And some homes are round, but they stand separately not aggregated. The squared-off shape uses space
most efficiently.

Automobiles and other modes of transportation are
not right angles. Boxy shape resists movement, so over time
strategic curves were added. Our bodies and the bodies of
all creatures are rounded—no straight lines. And it is our
rounded joints which allow bending to a right angle which
can cause us much pain.

Questions: do we tend to devise and construct
right-angle structures, or are we just doing straight lines? Is
a straight line always a sign that someone has been there?
Nature abhors a vacuum, perhaps nature also feels the
same way about a straight line!

Final question: What about roundabouts?

Why Write a Story or Memoir?

by Rosemary Hume

"Our journey through life includes many experiences and dimensions. The spiritual journey along our own unique pathway takes us through peaks, valleys, deserts, and storms. Our paths bring times when life is warm and blossoming and others that are cold and dry. We need to encourage each other as "travelers" on life's pathway and share the tools we have along the way."*

We are all in the process of formation. We give and receive form throughout our whole life. This formation process depends on cumulative wisdom that we pass from generation to generation. One generation alone cannot account for carrying on the spirit of a family or an organization. Storytelling, writing memoirs, or "tradition bearers" can inspire the people that read them. The writer or the teller contributes to one's individual or organization's history and to one's human spirit.

Recently we were talking with our grandson, who is in middle school. When we asked him what his favorite classes are in school, he mentioned his class on memoirs. He related that the students were reading a memoir and were going to write a memoir or story of their own. My husband and I had finished writing a book on our memoirs last year and our grandson shared it with the teachers.

This surprised us. Usually he says he likes math or "I don't know."

I decided to contact his teacher to ask her about the curriculum she was using with these middle school students. She says, "Reading stories about memoirs and then writing a memoir of their own helps our eighth graders learn to love to read and write." She has taught language arts for twenty years.

"Memoirs," she says, "don't go into someone's whole life story and state the facts as an autobiography does, but instead, they concentrate on an event/story or events/ stories that were important to the author. The students connect with memoirs because they usually focus on a particular theme or subject. They are able to empathize with the character and learn a valuable lesson or two. The story or memoir usually doesn't follow a plot diagram or a formal written pattern like a novel."

Laura Conklin, the teacher, said that it is wonderful for the senior generation to share their stories, especially for the younger generations to read. Our youth need to know what it was like back in the day and the real struggles and triumphs that people went through. She said that children today could really learn some valuable life lessons from previous generations.

So, why should you/we write a story or memoir? It can provide cumulative wisdom from our generation to the next generation. It can contribute to the formation of those who read the story. It can contribute to nourishing someone's human spirit.

Spirituality & Spiritual Formation: On the Path to Wholeness. Pamphlet 1996. Page 1.

Welcome to the 21st Century

by Don Grayson

Ugh!

I'm not sure I am ready for this century; the new cell phones have so many new features. Blue Teeth, Air Droop, Super Hyper Retina Delay, Voice Cognition, Ultra-wide waistband support, and a very small Wee Fly. Or maybe it's a travel aid, Why Fly?

Some of the features are even Virtually Real, whatever that means. The new cell phones are good up to 5G, even though I rarely exceed 1G, even in Airplane Mode. The APPS drive me crazy: Amazon, Twitter, and Facebook always have "suggestions" to sell me something.

And the abbreviations bother me. Is GPS a Geographic People Search? USB is obviously a Universal School Bus. God only knows what HTML stands for.

I miss turning the crank and saying, "Hello, Central?"

P.S. Sent from my iPad.

How I Met My Wife

by Bruce Hume

Those were the days, when it was likely that you would meet the person you would eventually marry in college. This is a story of persistence, love, and longevity.

In March 1963, during my last and senior year of college, I met my eventual wife. The event was at a bar called BEN'S Tavern. BEN'S has since burned down. I was there with another fraternity brother and about ten pledges after a fraternity work session.

While buying the pledges a soft drink or beer, I noticed that my younger fraternity brother was sitting in a dark corner of the bar talking to three young ladies. Now, in my fraternity culture, it would be discourteous to not invite an older "brother" over to the table. I just walked over and invited myself. I was attracted to one called Rosemary.

After talking a half hour or so, we noticed the other two ladies and my fraternity brother had left the bar. Perhaps they were bored by our conversation. In any case, after making sure the pledges knew how to get back to the fraternity house, I talked Rosemary (who everyone else called Rosie) into walking back across campus to get my car. Along the way, we noticed that *To Kill a Mockingbird* was playing at the State Street movie theater. We got my car and I drove Rosemary back to her apartment, which was on the same side of campus as BEN'S. The next night, I invited her to go see *To Kill a Mockingbird* on Saturday. She accepted.

That date was followed shortly by a formal dance at the fraternity and subsequent dates until I graduated in early June. I was slated to go to a management training program at AT&T Long Lines in Chicago. Then, at the end of June, I left for active duty in Lompoc, California, at Vandenberg Air Force Base. There I was to serve at the 6595th Aerospace Test Wing for the next three and one-half years.

Rosemary did not graduate until December 1963. We kept in touch by letter, phone, and one telegram. The phone bills became very expensive—forty percent of my air force income for the year was spent on long-distance phone calls.

While I was in Chicago, Rosemary went with a friend during summer break to New York City to tour and plan to move to New York to work in a hospital there.

In September, I returned home in route to Philadelphia. I stopped at home. I persuaded Rosemary to come visit California with the intent of potential marriage. In November, while at home for Thanksgiving, I went to meet Rosemary's family and asked her father if I could marry her. I also took Rosemary to meet my parents and extended family.

By Christmas, Rosemary had started to receive job offers from hospitals in Santa Barbara. I had gone to those hospitals to interview for a job for her. In January, Rosemary packed her possessions in boxes and moved one hundred forty-four pounds to Santa Barbara on a Greyhound bus.

She was met in the bus station by the director of nursing of Santa Barbara General Hospital. I was unable to meet her because we were working at the base around the clock because we didn't have enough engineers. I was forgiven for not meeting her and finally carried on our courtship in February.

We married in Ohio, in September. We spent our honeymoon at the New York World's Fair. The rest is history —three sons, Craig, Erik, and Dan; eight grandchildren— Madeline, Turner, Joe, Lily, Hannah, Haley, Ben and Dani. It is fifty-five years later and, by the grace of God, I made the right choice and I would do it all again.

Adaptive Re-Use at the Zoo

by Lucy Riegel

Recommended by Lucy Librarian

Warsaw Zoo, an unusual hiding place, was the jewel of Warsaw before the German occupation of Poland during World War II. It was esteemed by all zoo managers and aficionados of Europe and thus spared the worst treatment. Zookeepers Antonio and Jan Zabinski made good use of the animal enclosures for numerous "guests," mostly escaping Jews. Their nearby home provided more comfortable quarters for those able to hide in plain sight. And between their Villa and the zoo, there were underground rooms and tunnels.

Antonia managed to keep the Germans away with the combination of subterfuge and pleasantness. She built on prior relationships with German zookeepers, specialists who had been drafted by Hitler to create a showcase zoo and animal breeding program for Germany. She was clever enough to entertain German officers while "guests" hid in her home.

Somehow, she and her family and friends of the Polish underground conspired to provide food, shelter, and eventual escape for their "guests"—and also for the various lesser creatures who lived inside their home. A badger, a chicken, a monkey toddler, and a raven, for example.

Descriptions of daily life under German occupation and the horrors of the ghetto provide background. Reconstructions of Anthony's appreciation of nature, of animal life, and even recreations of prehistoric animals bred by Hitler's scientists complete the story.

This is a description of *The Zookeepers Wife* by Diane Ackerman, copyright 2007, nonfiction, Marquette library.

Doug

by Beverly Heid

A poignant recounting of a moment in life that had a big impact on a few who were involved and likely many more who were not.

Doug's obituary was in Sunday's paper. What a wonderful, talented man he was.

I met Doug only a few months ago at a social event at the retirement home where I live. I saw him get up on the stage to dance while I was playing the piano, entertaining the group. Doug was having such a good time he asked for more songs he could dance to. He set such an example with his skillful twists and turns that he was soon joined on stage by Charles, and then Billie.

People loved it! But later I was told not to play "dancing" songs. The staff was concerned that over-eager participants might fall, either walking between the tables to reach the stage or do so on the steps leading onto the stage.

"Who was this old man who loved to dance?" I thought. I soon found out.

Over time, my husband, Bob, and I enjoyed eating in the grill with Doug and his friend Walt. We learned that these two men were childhood friends. They were in Boy Scouts together. Both had families and they were now widowers. Doug lived on the second floor and Walt on the third.

Even at 90+ years, both Doug and Walt were physically active. Recently, I asked Walt about how Doug was doing. It appeared to me that the usually active Doug was slowing down.

Because of the unusual times we are facing due to the COVID-19 restrictions there have been many changes in our social lives. The last Friday social found me playing the piano on stage by myself! Me at the piano and the music was broadcast on channel 91 TV. Volunteers passed through the halls with a cart giving out popcorn in packages and bottled drinks for any resident who had opened their apartment door at the appointed hour.

Voila! Some residents have told me that they danced to the music in their apartments. Good creative thinking! I'm sure that would have included Doug but ...

We'll miss you, Doug!

#2197

by Marion Simpson

A memorable story from World War II. Marion R. Simpson was drafted into the United States Army in 1943 at the age of 19. He was transferred into the Army Air Corps, the forerunner of the Army Air Force, and became one of the original members of the air transport command (ATC). This unit was formed to move essential supplies and personnel to the area of need. He and his crew flew out of Miami, Florida, across the Atlantic, North Africa, the Middle East, and into India; supplying the Air Force, including those flying the "hump" into China. This is one of the events he remembers:

Another time, we left the Azores early in the evening for a long over-water flight to Bermuda. Normally this flight was about 14 hours without strong headwinds. As we passed the "point of no return," somewhere over the Bermuda Triangle, the aircraft engines began to sputter. Eventually all four engines quit. We were flying at just over 14,000 feet and went into a sharp downward glide.

The engineer was working frantically to restart the engines. Finally, he got two of them going. By that time, we were down to about 3,000 feet. The pilot pulled the plane out of the dive at 1,000 feet.

Shortly afterward, he got the other two started. We had no further problems and continued on to Bermuda. Several times on flights, I had noticed the same plane grounded at various stops. A few months later, as we were crossing the Atlantic, we made an approach to the runway at Ascencion Island. We were instructed to land on an alternate strip due to a crash on the main runway. After landing, we were told that the plane had no survivors. I casually mentioned it must have been #2197. Immediately, I was called up to the Provost Marshal's office and questioned.

They asked me, "How did you know the number of that crashed plane?" They told me that information had not been released. I explained the experience I had had on #2197 when all four engines had quit while we were flying from the Azores to Bermuda through the Bermuda Triangle. I also told them I'd seen #2197 several times, sidelined at various bases where we had landed. This must have satisfied the Provost Marshall. He told me I could go.

The science of predicting weather has come a long way since the 1940s. At that time, they couldn't track the path of the storm until it became a full hurricane. On one of the flights from Casablanca heading to the Azores, we picked up strong headwinds. This trip usually took approximately 6 hours flying time. We had been bucking headwinds since leaving Casablanca. By the time we approached the Azores, we had been in the air for 9 hours. We realized we were in the middle of a hurricane and that our destination, Lajes on the island of Terceira, in the Azores, was closed. We were instructed to proceed to Santa Marie Island. Conditions there were even worse. We were instructed to return to Lajes.

When we got there, the flight controller told us we couldn't possibly land! He said to ditch the plane in the ocean, and they would try to get a launch out to pick us up. Our captain said, "No way! We were coming in for a landing!"

At just that moment, lightning struck the plane, knocking out the radio, leaving us unable to communicate with the tower for further instructions. As we hit the runway, we skidded off onto the grass and stopped in the middle of the field. We had been in the air over 9 hours. When we measured the remaining gas in the plane, we found we had only 9 minutes of fuel left.

A Lifelong Love of the Accordion

by Fred Hecker

Sometimes things find us and other times we find things. This is the story of a boy and an accordion who found each other.

The Depression in the early 1930s was a hardship for many. My father, an electrician, sometimes had to go out of town for work. At one point, Mom, Dad, and I moved into my grandparents' home. It was never explained to me why the move, but I think it was for financial reasons. Later, we moved back into the house we had been renting and where I was born.

Prior to Christmas 1936, I came home from first grade with a picture of a Christmas tree and a box under the tree. Of course, the question was, "What's in the box?" I said it was an accordion. Back then, accordions were as popular as guitars are today.

Since my father was also a musician, I think he felt that the accordion was an ideal Christmas present. The "box" contained a small 12-bass accordion, a size ideal for a young child.

Lessons followed and, of course, practicing. Sometimes, practicing was easy. When it was a harder piece of music, I preferred playing outside with my neighborhood friends.

I eventually progressed to a bigger-sized accordion. The lessons continued and I became more proficient, but not perfect.

Mother was active in the church's Lady's Society and she asked me to provide accordion. So, I dutifully played a respectable song. When they asked for an encore, the first song that came to my mind, which I readily knew, was not a church hymn, but the "Beer Barrel Polka." Nevertheless, the ladies enjoyed it.

During my Junior High School days (grades 7-8-9), I started playing the trumpet in the school band. The trumpet was the same instrument that my father played. During this time, I occasionally played the accordion. Being outside with neighborhood kids was more fun.

One summer, between my 9th and 10th grades, I restarted practicing and acquired quite a repertoire. Around my junior and senior years in high school, I joined a three-piece orchestra and continued playing during my first year in college. It was the University of Wisconsin extension division in my hometown of Manitowoc, Wisconsin, where I spent one year. Of course, I had to join the Musician's Union. The money earned went a long way toward college expenses.

Next, I went to Madison, Wisconsin, for on-campus enrollment. There, I had fun playing at fraternity parties and for fellow pharmacy classmates at a local tavern.

During my senior year in Madison, the football team won the Big 10 title, which meant the team would be going to the Rose Bowl on January 1, 1953. Alan Ameche, running back, was the star player and eventually became a Colt in Baltimore.

I decided to make the trip to the Rose Bowl. Our journey was by train from Madison to Los Angeles. I do not remember exactly, but it was a 2-to-3-day trip each way. My trusty accordion accompanied me on the trip. I would play from railroad car to another "On Wisconsin" and "California Here I Come." The playing continued in the Club car.

As a pharmacy student, with the class I visited pharmaceutical companies like Abbott in North Chicago and Lilly in Indianapolis. During a banquet at the Abbott visit, we were entertained by strolling musicians, one of whom played the accordion. Not being bashful, I asked if I could play it, which I did. Later, the accordionist said he was getting a new accordion. Would I be interested in his accordion? We finalized a deal and I was the proud owner of a professional accordion.

That accordion helped me earn money playing with an orchestra during my grad school days. Courtship was limited, as I was likely playing on Saturday night. In retrospect, I earned money, rather than spending it on a date. My future bride understood.

Now, I play for entertainment at Marquette in Assisted Living and in Reflections (memory care). My wife, Alice, currently is a resident in Reflections.

The accordion I acquired in college was showing its age. I took it to the accordion doctor, and I said it had asthma—it was wheezing. The repair person said he did his best and suggested it might be time to look for a different accordion. After all, it had been good to me for 67 years.

Ever since my high school days, I admired the Excelsior brand, which was played by some of the leading players of the day. I went to eBay and lo and behold, I found a very professional Excelsior.

So, I am now realizing my childhood dream. I have been playing since the age of 6 and soon I will be 90 years young. What turned out to be in the "box" under the Christmas tree, has provided a source of pleasure and income.

Buying a Car

by Ed Koskie

Buying a new car is always exciting and even more so when it has novel features.

It started in 1999, when I saw the first iteration of the Toyota Hybrid in a parking lot on the Cape. I had already seen and examined the GM EV-1 while I was volunteering at the Crawford Auto Museum in Cleveland, Ohio. The EV-1 was the first attempt of General Motors at production of an all-electric driven car. The Museum's car was one that GM disabled the motor so it could not be driven but be on display to illustrate the concept. It was a new, very neat-looking coupe and fired the idea of a "green" car supporting the environment growing in my mind. As a side note, as with the EV-1, GM has often found itself having leading technology coming out of engineering only to be killed by the financial domination of HQ.

In 2005, my first wife's car gave up the ghost unexpectedly and she needed a new car pronto. The Hybrid Toyota Prius was starting production and we (actually I) drooled at the design but the delivery was out almost a year, so we settled on a Camry that came off the dealer's floor. As time went on, I followed the emergence of the Prius, but my wife's deteriorating physical condition and need for transporting a wheelchair dictated a larger car with adequate trunk capacity. After her death and the need for reorienting my life's direction, the idea of another car took a backseat.

Arriving at Marquette, the twin ideas of a new car and latest technology began to slowly bubble up in the back of my mind. Just about the time I started to become serious about a hybrid, however, cars with all-electric drive started to show up. Tesla introduced a roadster but that was way too expensive for my pocketbook. Then came the Mod S, but still the cost was far beyond any conceivable justification. Tesla next recognized that to be a viable manufacturer they needed a more affordable entry. Hence, the Mod 3. Also, Chevrolet, Nissan, and others introduced fully-electric driven cars and the race seemed to be on.

The flame was growing within me, but I needed to exhibit caution and be sure the technology as well as the price was right. Sometimes being an engineer gets in the way of dreams! I needed a push.

At last Christmas, Nancy's son David visited, as did my daughter Sarah. While both were here, we had a brainstorm: "Let's go look at a Tesla!" Both thought that was a good idea. Little did they know that the dam was being breached.

Each suggested, "Isn't it time to shake loose some of the money that had been gathering over the years?" So, shortly thereafter, Nancy and I arranged for a test drive. Do you know what happens to an old codger when he is thrown back into the seat by mere slight depression of the throttle? Especially when your wife says, "Quit that!"

Well, all caution was gone. All prudent ideas of financial payback calculations were gone. All discretionary spending ideas were out the window. The insane idea of buying a Tesla as a birthday present for my 90th birthday seemed the most logical and sane thing I have ever done.

The Tesla Model 3 delivery was on March 20.

The Cup of Sorrow

by Margaret Hall Simpson

After 40 years on a shelf, the true identity of the cup is revealed.

Many years ago, a hospice patient gave me an enamel beaker with what looked like Russian symbols, the date 1896, and some initials on the side. It was not particularly attractive and had some nicks in the rim, but my patient said she had treasured it for many years and wanted me to have it. I took it home and forgot about it.

Several years later, I was looking through an *Arts and Antiques* magazine and saw a small picture of a cup that looked familiar. The accompanying article gave a brief history of the cup and called it "The Cup of Sorrow."

Sometime later, I found the enameled beaker on a shelf in my home, with pens and pencils in it. My curiosity was aroused. I entered "Cup of Sorrow" in the computer and the story of this old cup was there: To celebrate the coronation of Tsar Nicholas II and Tsarina Alexandra Feodorovna on May 18, 1896, gifts of silk scarves with the names of the Tsar and Tsarina, and ornately decorated enameled cups, were to be distributed to the guests. This white cup had the initials of Nicholas and Alexandra surrounded by a geometric pattern and the Romanov eagle on the opposite side.

The Cup of Sorrow

In addition to the gifts, food and beer was to be distributed to the crowd of peasants gathered on Khodynka Field to witness the coronation. This was a training ground with pits and trenches dotting the entire field. More than half a million people were crowded together on the field. More people than could be safely accommodated. The supply of food and beer was not sufficient for the size of the gathering. The crowd, already restive, went wild when a rumor passed quickly through the crowd that the commemorative enamel cups had a gold coin in the bottom. A stampede ensued and, in the melee, 1,389 people were trampled to death and another 1,300 injured.

An elaborate Coronation Ball was planned for that evening. Advisors to the Tsar urged Nicholas to cancel the festivities in light of the tragedy or refrain from attending. Nicholas willfully attended the splendid occasion, accompanied by Alexandra. For his callous behavior, he earned the nickname "Bloody Nicholas."

This became known as the Khodynka Tragedy and the enameled cup called The Cup of Sorrow or The Cup of Tears. This tragic event was considered an omen for the reign of Tsar Nicholas II.

Nicholas II, the last Tsar of Russia, was an ineffectual leader, more interested in his family life and his own pursuits than in ruling Russia. Alexandra, granddaughter of England's Queen Victoria, being of strong character, tried to make Nicholas into a more capable leader without success. She was hated by the Russian people and during the war with Germany she was called "The German Woman."

After twenty-four years as Tsar of Russia, Nicholas and his wife, Alexandra; four daughters and one son; their servants; dogs; and anyone who had accompanied them when they were imprisoned, were murdered on July 17, 1918, by order of the Ural Regional Soviet.

The Last Goodbye

by Barbara Furlow

The times we live in stir emotions.

"See ya Monday!" That doesn't sound like a last goodbye. Yet those are the words echoing across a seventy-year span. My college friend Jackie had lucked out with a ride home to New Orleans for the weekend, while I had to take the bus.

Although my mother tried, there was no easy, gentle way for her to waken me the next morning with the news that Jackie was dead, killed in a horrific car crash some forty miles south of Baton Rouge.

Her infectious grin—a switch, lighting her sparkling green eyes. Her laugh, a bubble—growing until everyone around her was somehow drawn into the fun.

That was Jackie, so alive, so very alive. And I didn't get to say goodbye.

During this past six months, there are so many to whom we didn't get to say goodbye. It has been so difficult, so cold, so lonely, not to say goodbye ... and yet, you know that you cannot say goodbye unless you first said, hello.

Can you remember some of your first hellos here? Think about it. See the face. Feel your own tentative smile as you remember saying hello to someone new. Many of us moved in knowing at least a few people; and as we looked around, walked the halls, went to dinner, became acclimated, we realized a treasure trove of friendships were just waiting to be made, all starting with that first hello. Picture again the very first person who said hello to you the day you moved in ...

Jim's accent fell on my Southern ears, turning hello into a refrain from Sinatra's "New York, New York." We worked together to select the marker stones that tell you how far you've walked. J.J. often reminded me that I was the first person to say hello to him when he moved in. He was so tall, and I'm still shrinking. Bob's gentle grin—how I miss that wonderfully warm feeling just seeing him smile. Rose, tiny, mighty, twinkling like starlight. Tom, surely the whole world said hello to Tom; well, okay, maybe not the whole world. Pat Peterson, his hello—and so much more. Pat discovered I was an avid golfer. And I discovered Pat wasn't even a golfer, but he was the person responsible for *Golf Digest* showing up in my mailbox. He said it made him happy to see me happy. More than forty years ago, I had first hellos and the gift of enduring friendship with Helen and Lynn and knowing they were always there for me, the epitome of Kahlil Gibran's "friendship being your needs answered."

As you hear these names, do you remember some special moment that made your life richer? Because of the pandemic, you may be feeling a deep sadness at the missed opportunity of saying goodbye, of letting friends know the gift they were in your life. So today, please find comfort in knowing how blessed your life and theirs was because of your first hello.

Yes, it was seventy years ago that Jackie died, and her smile, her laugh, her presence are just as real today. Perhaps I just ...

The Last Goodbye

Always thought I'd say goodbye
not that I wanted you to go,
but, of course, I knew you would, everyone does
but I always thought I'd say goodbye.

I always thought I'd say goodbye
some long-held thought, some wit or wisdom
those words I wanted you to hear
but I always thought I'd say goodbye.

I always thought I'd say goodbye
we were so close, you and I
the places we'd been, the memories we shared
and I always thought I'd say goodbye.

I always thought I'd say goodbye
now you are gone and I, I am here
filled with the echo of our first hello
So, I think I'll never ever say goodbye.

June 29, 2020

Boom!

by Beverly Heid

Seventy-four people were killed and nearly 400 were injured at a "Holiday on Ice" show in Indianapolis on October 31, 1963. Here are the words of a survivor of the blast that occurred at 11:00 PM, three minutes from the end of the show.

The skaters were facing the audience for the grand finale. Suddenly, we felt our seats jerk. Flames shot up in front of us and bodies were flying. In the confusion, I tried to reach a man who I thought was my husband. Then my husband grabbed me and we headed for an exit.

We climbed over debris. The first doors were locked. I lost my shoes and coat. Where did our mothers go? Where were Bob's sister and husband?

Little did we know that we had been sitting atop popcorn tanks that were leaking the gas and had exploded. The flames went out. They said our seats collapsed after we got away. The people sitting in front of us had been seated on folding chairs. Those chairs and people were thrown onto the ice.

We made our way to the car. Both of our mothers, and Karen and Ken also, made it out of the carnage. We could see the flames and thought the entire coliseum was afire.

Boom!

The following morning, the newspaper had the story. Our friends who knew where we were sitting thought we had been killed. People on the other side of the rink could see that the explosion was localized.

As the day went on, we realized we were in a state of shock. We were lucky survivors.

Hagia Sophia, A Missed Opportunity

by Jackie King

Sound advice from an experienced traveler.

In 1994, Art and I traveled to Istanbul, Turkey. We spent a week in the city; I attended a conference and after hours we toured the city. We took advantage of trips on the Bosphorus, picnics on the Asian side, tours of the Domabache and Topkapi Palaces, and other sights. We had a friend with us who had lived in Turkey and knew how to find interesting places inside the city that most tourists would not find.

It was an exciting and exhausting week. One day we toured the famous Blue Mosque, just across a square from Hagia Sophia. Afterward, we sat outside in a café, looking at our next place to visit, Hagia Sophia. The longer we looked at the site, the more comfortable we became just sitting and enjoying the street scene.

It had been a week of nonstop meetings and touring and we were wearing out fast. We looked at each other and decided to tour Hagia Sophia on our next trip to Istanbul; we bought a postcard and took a taxi back to our hotel and left the next day.

What a missed opportunity! We haven't been back and are not putting Istanbul on our return list.

From the *Washington Post* on July 13, 2020:

Hagia Sophia, built by the Emperor Justinian I in 537, was once the largest and grandest church in all of Christendom and remains at the spiritual heart of Orthodox Christianity. ... It was converted into a mosque in 1453, when the Ottomans conquered Istanbul, with minarets placed around its perimeter, its byzantine mosaics covered in whitewash... A 1934 decree by Turkey's secularist modern founder, Mustafa Kemal Ataturk, made Hagia Sophia into a museum that commemorated the depth of this countries history, which predates the advent of Islam. It became a monument to a universal legacy that transcends religion and underscored Istanbul's place at the heart of different cultures and faiths ... Until Friday, when the Turkish president announced that Hagia Sophia would be a mosque again, with Muslim prayers resuming in the compound in two weeks. Turkish officials said the site would remain open to all and that its Christian icons and mosaics would not be damaged."

Well, it is hard to be confident that things will go as stated above. Based on this experience, I urge fellow travelers to overcome inertia and fatigue and see the sights when you visit places. Don't wait until next time, there may not be one!

Try Your Hand At ...

by The Editors

Writing a story can be fun.

Since you are checking out this week's Chapbook, it is likely that you find this feature worth your time. There have been 40 of these interesting stories written by more than a dozen different people like you, readers and friends. Some share interesting stories from their lives. Others discuss things like right angles or what the 21st century means to them. And some have contributed to the Poets' Corner. All it takes is an idea and a willingness to share.

You ask yourself, "Should I try?" If the answer is yes, go for it! You may have done something like this before, or it could be your first time. You do not have to be a polished writer, just have a willingness to share.

All that is required from you is a Word document of about 500 words sent as an email attachment. Don't worry excessively about punctuation, spelling, or even grammar. We can help with that. Write as you would speak, telling your story. Then, send the Word document as an attachment to: yourgoodlife84@gmail.com

Let us know if you need help. We look forward to hearing from you.

A Moment Can Last Forever

by Barbara R. Furlow

Who knew that a moment, seemingly insignificant, would be indelibly imprinted for a lifetime. It was just a poem, words on paper. Yet it became a mantra of calm when frightened, energy when weakened, comfort when saddened, hope when despairing.

Twenty-one, recently married, and newly settled in an apartment complex housing Fort Benning's basic infantry officers' fall class of 1954, life was good. We were all young, new to the active military and to each other.

For the men, most of them recent graduates of West Point, training was grueling, studies were rigorous; free time was scarce. With money almost as scarce, Saturday entertainment was a game of Canasta with two other couples. Every other Saturday, we'd pile in cars and drive to the Kinnett Dairy ice-cream parlor for our really big splurge, a banana split or hot fudge sundae.

One Saturday, Bill and Loretta mentioned that a bishop they had known in New York was serving as Interim Pastor at the big Methodist Church in downtown Columbus. Their enthusiastic description of his preaching led to the spontaneous decision that we would all go to the 11 o'clock services.

It seemed as if everyone in town made the same decision. We had to sit on wooden folding chairs on the church lawn. After this, getting to church early each Sunday for a bulletin and a seat inside became a priority.

A Moment Can Last Forever

On one of those Sundays, Bishop Cushman had printed a poem he had written as a part of the sermon in the bulletin.

The joy in his voice resonated with the need in my spirit for the simple wisdom which, as Robert Frost would say, "has made all the difference." It has echoed through living in Germany; through miscarriages; through childbirth; through my grandmother's death and never saying goodbye; through a brief television career; through 17 moves; through family illnesses and sleepless nights; through divorce; through studying in China; through success and sorrow; and yes, even now in old age and the pandemic. Because ...

I met God in the morning
When my day was at its best,
And His presence came like sunrise,
Like a glory in my breast.

All day long the Presence lingered,
all day long He stayed with me,
And we sailed in perfect calmness
O'er a very troubled sea.

Other ships were blown and battered,
Other Ships were sore distressed,
But the winds that seemed to drive them,
Brought to us a peace and rest.

Then I thought of other mornings,
With a keen remorse of mind,
When I too had loosed the moorings,
With the Presence left behind.

So I think I know the secret,
Learned from many a troubled way

A Moment Can Last Forever

You must seek God in the morning
If you would have him through your day.

—Ralph Spaulding Cushman

Indeed, Bishop, it has made all the difference.

Long-Overdue Family Reunion

by Federico Dies

Families might lose track of each other, but bonds in this family were kindled thanks to an unusual name.

This is a story of a long-overdue family reunion and discovery that is both true and somewhat unusual.

My great-grandparents, Antonio Dies and Antonia Matarredona, lived in Valencia, Spain, and had five children. For this story I will focus on two of them: José, my grandfather, and his brother Francisco. José moved to Alicante, a province of Valencia, married Guillermina Terol, and they had six children. One of those children, my father, was named Haroldo, a very unusual name in Spain. My father's family moved to Madrid when he was still a teenager and did not keep any ties to their relatives in Valencia City that they had left. They only kept some vague recollection of the existence of their family.

My father, Haroldo Dies, married Pilar Angulo in Madrid in 1931. They moved to Paris, France, in 1935, where I was born the following year. Because of the Civil War in their native Spain and the imminent German invasion of France, my parents, with me in tow, sought asylum in Mexico in 1940.

Two years later, my brothers, Guillermo and Haroldo,

117

were born in Mexico City on the same day, fifteen minutes apart—identical twins. In time, Guillermo became a chemical engineer and Haroldo a physician specializing in diabetes.

My grandfather's brother, Francisco, remained in Valencia, married Casilda Diaz, and had five children. Their fourth child, also named Francisco, is our focus on this side of the larger Dies family. He became a lawyer and accountant in Valencia and married Amparo Gil. They had two boys named Francisco (the third in a row with that popular Spanish name in his family) and Haroldo, the first so named in his town, if not the region, or even the country —an unusual name. For many years there was no contact between those two branches of Antonio Dies' family.

The third-generation descendants lived in different regions of the country at first, and then in different countries. There was some vague knowledge on my father's part that the family was much larger than we knew.

In the mid-1990s, a newspaper in Valencia, Spain, published news from Mexico that Bishop Samuel Ruiz, who had gained fame as a mediator between warring factions in Mexico, had fallen ill from complications of diabetes and was under the care of my brother Dr. Haroldo Dies-Angulo. Upon reading this news, brothers Francisco and Haroldo Dies-Gil, my cousins living in Spain, were amazed. They knew from family lore that there had been a Dies family member named Haroldo who had traveled to America. This was such a remarkable family event that one of them had been named Haroldo after that adventurous, almost mythic relative. When the cousins came out of their amazement, they said to each other: "This doctor in Mexico has to be family!"

So, they took what appeared to be the most expeditious step at the time and they wrote a letter to Dr. Haroldo Dies, my brother, in care of Bishop Samuel Ruiz, San Cristobal de las Casas, Chiapas, Mexico, identifying themselves and asking relevant obvious questions.

Their letter reached Bishop Ruiz and he relayed the letter inside to my brother. We all read the letter at my parents' home and immediately understood who these cousins were: the descendants from our grandfather's brother. After that, things proceeded smoothly. Of course, we replied to their letter, identified ourselves with appropriate detail, and made plans to travel to Spain. Shortly after we arrived in Madrid, we took a rapid train to Valencia City. We had advised our "new" cousins of the time when we would be arriving in Valencia.

When we disembarked the train, our group included five: my mother (my father passed away the previous year); my brother Guillermo; his wife, Eva; my wife, Rosa Maria; and I (brother Haroldo could not come this time). We were met on the station's platform by no less than fifty members of the Dies clan who were descendants of our great-grandfather Antonio Dies.

They cheered, we cried, and all had the best conceivable reunion as we moved to the home of one of the new cousins. We met on a large lawn with a canopy, tables for food, and a pool for the younger cousins to swim. We ate "paella," the traditional dish from Valencia. It was the best we have had to this date. We drank good Valencian wine and we talked like we hadn't seen each other since last Sunday.

There was great chemistry and we have maintained the relationship through letters, emails, Facebook, and occasional in-person visits to this date. They are also going through the corona virus pandemic with social distancing, masks, and hygiene; while maintaining a relatively good mood and patience, but thankfully without major complications. It is a great feeling being a member of such a large family and keeping up with all of them is more than worth the effort and time.

Widow Lessons (Part 1)

by Margaret Hall Simpson

When my husband and I were married in 1955, I expected I was going to be a *traditional housewife*. (Husband bringing home the bacon, wife at home to cook it). I had quit my job at a bank and was prepared to cook, clean house, do laundry, and wait for the babies. My new, easy-going husband had a slightly different slant on how our marriage was going to shape up. He said he was going to give me *widow lessons*. That was a scary thought for a new bride. Did he have some premonition he was going to die and leave me a young widow?

No premonition. He just wanted me to be aware of our financial situation and be able to function on my own if necessary. Before we were married, he had bought a house for us to move into when we got back from our honeymoon. He made sure I knew how much our income was and an idea how it was to be spent. I knew how much the mortgage was, what portion of each payment went to principal, and how much to interest. I had a grocery budget and knew when to pay the bills: gas, water, electricity, taxes and how much to put in a savings account.

As I became adept at handling household finances, he added more widow lessons. I was then expected to be responsible for the maintenance of the family car: oil change, tires rotated, water in the radiator, anti-freeze in winter, and the gas tank filled. Keeping the gas tank filled was the big problem. About that time, gas stations began to be self-service. You no longer drove up and the attendant came out, you rolled down the window and said "fill-er up" and he would clean the windshield and check the oil level while the gas was running in. Now you had to pump your own gas. I hated that! I thought it was the most un-feminine task a woman could be asked to do. I would drive to the station, check to see if anyone I knew was around before I would get out of the car and start (ugh) pumping.

Next added to my job description was taking the car in for repairs. I dreaded that too and would procrastinate as long as possible. The first time I took the car in, the man in the front of the shop asked, "What may I do for you?"

I said, "My car needs to be fixed."

He said, "What exactly is the car doing that it shouldn't be doing?"

I said, "I don't know, that's why I brought it to you."

His smile grew wider. He said, "Can you give me a little more information?"

I said, "It's making a funny noise."

"What sort of noise" he asked.

"Thumpledy-thump" I said. "Or maybe it sounds more like rattledy-whack under the hood."

The man excused himself and went into the glass enclosure where several men in cover-alls were standing. They all turned and looked out at me, laughing their heads off. I wanted to sink into the concrete floor.

The front-man came back out and said, "I'm afraid you will have to leave the car and one of our mechanics who is a specialist in "thumpeldy-thump and rattledy-whack" will examine it. We will call you after we find out what is causing your problem."

I flew out of there with my face burning.

I eventually learned enough about automobiles to at least describe the problem to a mechanic. All part of the widow lessons.

But there was more ...

More Widow Lessons (Part 2)

by Margaret Hall Simpson

As time went on, I learned how to buy major appliances, get estimates on home repairs, and acquire cemetery lots. All this happened while I learned to cook, sew, knit, and have a baby. With this addition to the family, we outgrew the first house and I learned what to look for when house hunting and how to deal with real estate salesmen.

Next, husband thought I should know how to buy a new car. I really didn't want to do this alone. Husband insisted. I would slip into a dealership, trying not to attract the attention of the sales staff. I just wanted to look at the cars and read the window stickers—but always got caught! A smiling salesman would materialize and begin questioning me about what kind of car I was interested in, price range, color, and if I had a car to trade in. I would say I would know when I saw the car I wanted. I visited a lot of dealerships, read lots of window stickers, and sat in a lot of new cars. Finally, I got up the courage to ask to test drive a car.

This became my new pastime. I drove every car from the top of the line to the basic stripped-down models. I could tell you about cylinders, horsepower, miles per gallon, tire size, leather or cloth seats, and whether a particular model had a cup holder. I was ready to talk to the salesman about cost and trade-in allowance.

This part went well and I even sat and listened to his presentation about the merits of leasing the automobile over buying it outright. I said no to leasing, paid cash, and drove my new Oldsmobile home. Another notch on my *widow lessons*.

In my middle age, I inherited my older brother's estate. This included a house that was over a hundred years old and some money. This brought on how to invest the money and whether to keep the house or sell it. Another *widow lesson* was in stocks, bonds, annuities, and real estate versus putting the money under the mattress.

Husband decides I should study the stock market and make my own decisions as to how I would invest what money was left after the inheritance taxes were paid. I made some mistakes but managed to make a few good investments. Then I had to decide what to do with the house. It was a big, old, twelve-room Victorian that I had grown up in, located in a small town in southern Indiana.

The house needed serious repairs whether I sold it or kept it. Husband says it's my decision. We still had the first house we lived in, which was now a rental; a cabin in the woods near Spencer, Indiana; and the house we presently lived in. That would make four. We definitely didn't need another house.

The old house I inherited needed a new roof. I got estimates and had the roof done. Husband does not offer any help with the project. Right! Another *widow lesson!* It was a grueling year-long adventure. I acted as my own general contractor and completely gutted and restored the house. I made lots of mistakes, but along the way I learned a lot. The house had so many wonderful memories I decided not to sell it.

Now, we are here.

By that time, our daughter had grown up, gone to college, taken a teaching job in Arizona, and gotten married.

We started thinking about down-sizing. Would we stay in our house, buy a smaller house, or go into an apartment? Some of our friends were moving into senior living facilities at that time and these senior facilities were popping up like mushrooms.

We began looking around while we discussed the pros and cons of spending the rest of our lives in a place that offered independent apartments and, when needed, assisted living and healthcare all under one roof. After much investigation and comparison, we decided on a place that would meet our needs and put our name on a waiting list until an apartment that fit our needs became available. We sold the house we had lived in for forty years and entered a senior living facility. End of *widow lessons*? No.

One day husband hands me a folder headed "Death Procedures." It contained lists: healthcare powers of attorney, living wills, who to call first when one of us dies, names and addresses of all family members, mortuary and burial instructions, who to contact regarding pension benefits, social security, name of attorney, list of bank accounts, brokerage accounts, trust papers, tax forms for previous three years, lists of bequests of personal items not specified in the trust, disposal of contents of apartment when last one dies. The list may not be complete yet. As we think of other things that would make it easier for the survivor, we will add them.

Yes, *widow lessons*.

Opportunity Still Knocks

by Lynda Smallwood

A late baby boomer or early generation X speaks to the generations that have preceded hers.

This is a heartfelt tribute to you who have gone before. You are the trailblazers of life; and yet, for you, opportunity still knocks. You worked hard to gain the wisdom and life experience you now possess. It has not been easy. There were tall mountains to climb and deep valleys to cross. There were unexpected twists and turns along the way. And yet, you made it through and stand now as a beacon to those of us who come along behind. But opportunity still knocks.

You remember the days when fruits and vegetables were grown in the ground by average families, when chickens were raised for eggs and slain for dinner. You have memories of supporting the war efforts during World War II; traveling by car over narrow state highways before the large national interstates were built; walking to school, to church, and to the corner store in your own neighborhoods where you grew up.

You remember the excitement of the first family TV that replaced radio as the source for news and entertainment, along with many other new inventions that changed the world we live in. And you were part of the space race, putting a man on the moon. You also remember when polio, measles, and other diseases were rampant before vaccines and cures were found. Not dwelling on the good ole days, you managed to find your way along in the new manner of life too. And opportunity still knocks.

You may sometimes feel unnoticed and unappreciated as the world around you speeds at a maddening pace. Sadly, that is often true. But there are some of us who pause from time to time and consider the impact of your generation upon our lives. Others of us may not stop to think about it until after you are gone, and only then realize that we missed the opportunity to learn so much from you. And perhaps even more of us will be so caught up in the daily grind of living, we never really come to understand that you were the trailblazers. That last group are the ones who will miss out the most. But opportunity still knocks!

There is still an opportunity for you to share with us what you have learned along the way. The youngest generation, who only remembers life when there were buttons to be pushed to get the desired results for food, news, or entertainment, can greatly benefit from your experience and perspective. So can those of us who lived somewhere in between the oldest and the youngest generations.

You have stories to tell of what it takes to overcome the challenges of life, to adapt to the change, and to rise above adversity. The specific details of daily living may have changed over time, with advances in medicine and technology, but the underlying themes remain the same. Do not lose sight of what it took to get you here. It is very reassuring to hear from those of you who dealt with challenges in the past and overcame them. It gives us courage to keep moving forward and do the same.

Opportunity is still knocking. What are you waiting for? We need to hear your stories—so share with us today!

Lifetime of Love & Saved Haircut Fees

by Federico Dies

Most "home" haircuts are one and done. This one lasted a lifetime.

Back in August of 1962, Rosa Maria and I got married in Mexico City in a hurry. There was no baby hurry, but we had to be at the U of R in Rochester, New York, before the end of the month to meet the chairman of the Department of Physiology, who was going to be my supervisor as a graduate student, because he was leaving for a sabbatical semester in Nigeria. We made it on time and I got started with courses, while Rosa Maria attended some English classes at the University.

A few weeks later, I had my first haircut ever outside of Mexico City at the corner barber shop; and the result was less than OK. So, for my second haircut, I recruited my wife for the task. She accepted somewhat reluctantly, borrowed an electric clipper and proceeded to run it through my hair with enthusiasm but without a second thought.

I didn't need another haircut for the next two or three months!

Then we purchased some stylist scissors at the drugstore and she started a lifelong career of monthly, carefully done, and increasingly elegant haircuts.

To this date, she has cut my hair about once a month for the fifty-eight years of our marriage, minus two haircuts a year when we visit family in either Chicago or Mexico City, or when we vacation in Cancun, where there are professional stylists that I like and trust.

Doing a little arithmetic, all this comes out to 12 haircuts per year x 58 years of marriage = 696 haircuts; minus 2 haircuts per year x 58 years = 116 haircuts. The grand total is 580 haircuts times an estimated $15 per haircut: I owe my wife $8,700 just for her efforts.

The real plus of this domestic arrangement is that I can get a haircut while in a quarantine whenever there is a pandemic and keep looking well groomed.

I do have to make an appointment, but I don't have to wear a mask!

It Took an Eagle Eye

by The Editors

An article from the Associated Press was spied by Marion Harcourt ,who then shared this story with us, the editors, of "Your Good Life."

A bald eagle attacked a drone sent aloft by the Michigan Department of Environment, Great Lakes, and Energy—destroying a propeller and causing the vehicle to crash in the waters of Lake Michigan. (According to the Michigan Department of Natural Resources, eagles have been making a "resurgence" in the past several decades. There are said to be 800 nesting pairs in the state.)

The incident occurred on a bright midsummer day as the drone was recording shoreline erosion near Escanaba in Michigan's Upper Peninsula. Information obtained from this effort would tell the effects of current high-water levels and help communities cope with the damage resulting.

Experts and the drone pilot said only seven minutes of the mapping flight had been completed when reports back from the drone became spotty. Attempts to retrieve the drone failed. On a video screen, the device costing $950, began to twirl.

"It was a bumpy roller-coaster ride," said the drone operator, who looked up and saw an eagle flying away, apparently unhurt by its confrontation with this alien flying machine.

Two birdwatchers who were nearby reported seeing the bird attack something but they didn't realize it was a drone.

The drone sent multiple warning notifications as it spiraled to the water, including a report that a propeller was missing. Although search of the shoreline failed to find the drone, analysis of data later revealed that it landed in four feet of water about 150 feet offshore.

The drone team is considering ways to reduce the chance of a repeat attack. These include other designs on the aircraft to make them look less like a seagull.

Miracles Really Can Happen

by Joe Helveston

One man's appreciation for the gift of sight.

Being born the youngest in a family of four boys
is not the best place to begin life. Trying to keep up with
the high standards and goals my brothers set in their lives
was a challenge. But this is not what I am writing about.
It is the vision condition I was saddled with that affected
many experiences in my life.

At the age of four, my parents took me to an eye doctor.
They watched me squinting while I held picture books so
close, they were almost touching my nose.

After a complete exam, the doctor explained to my
parents I was very farsighted and had an extreme astigmatism in both my eyes. After this, he prescribed glasses,
saying they would make my vision near normal, but only
if I wore them full-time—first thing in the morning till the
last thing at night.

Some of the children in school referred to the glasses
I wore as "Coke-bottle glasses." When they called me four
eyes, it usually resulted in a fight. Let me add at this point
that no one was ever hurt, and after the skirmish we usually made up after these brief hostilities.

During summer vacation, the City of Detroit Parks and

Recreation supported baseball leagues at the various parks in the area. My brothers played some and encouraged me to join a team. I remember standing in the outfield watching the batter hit the ball, only to see it disappear as I waited for it to come to me. By the time I caught sight of the ball I was not close enough to catch it. I was stationed in right field, except when a left-handed batter was up, then I was moved to left field. Not a vote of confidence! Let's just say playing for the Detroit Tigers was not on my list of future goals for life.

When I turned fourteen, one of my first jobs was caddy at a local country club. My brothers had been caddies and were considered good. The good caddies always carried the bags for the "best" players. These were not the ones who got the lowest scores. Oh no, they were the players higher up on the social scale and the biggest tippers (these traits were almost mutually exclusive).

Let me explain what makes a good caddie. First and most important, the caddie must know where the golf ball went after the player hits it off the tee. The next was carrying the clubs, and I had no problem with that. However, knowing where the ball went was a big problem. This was like looking for the baseball after it was hit in the air. The players I caddied for were not the big tippers.

My oldest brother served in The U.S. Army in the artillery during the Korean War. After I joined the Army at eighteen, my platoon sergeant asked me during basic training where I wanted to train. I told him, the artillery. My score on the rifle range was three points above passing. This didn't mean much because I believe the guys keeping score were told to be sure EVERYONE passed.

When I got my orders, they were for medic school. I believe the Army did not want me to carry anything that might harm someone. Experiences like this throughout my life, affected the way I felt about those glasses that have made my life "quite livable" in the words of the first eye doctor.

Please understand, I did well with the various challenges that I met. That is, until approaching eighty, when my vision was getting blurry despite glasses and contact lenses. The reason? Like nearly everyone who reaches this age, I was developing cataracts.

When I arranged to have cataract surgery, I was told by the team in the ophthalmologist's office that several different procedures were available for a person who had an astigmatism like mine. One of them was a toric lens that could be implanted in my eyes to make it possible for me to see with normal vision without the need for glasses. Added to this would be a small "relaxing" incision in the cornea. These extra procedures were not covered by Medicare but the promise of normal vision without glasses after surgery made the extra cost worth it.

When I get up in the morning is when it really hits me. For seventy-six years, the first thing I did every morning was put on my glasses so I could see properly. The reality hit me when I woke up—and just like that, I could see!! An operation on each eye that took minutes and a post-operative period with no pain and only the mild inconvenience of using drops for a few days made this possible.

I realize the procedure and the special lenses are the result of advancement in medical technology and a surgeon's skill—but to me, this has been a miracle.

A Lesson

by Ed Koskie

An act of kindness and a lesson learned.

A lesson for today. Many years ago, I was transferred to Forrest City, Arkansas (named after Confederate General Nathan Bedford Forrest), to be the engineering manager at the Yale Hoist manufacturing plant. Our children were about seven and nine years old. We were doing our best to give them a broad education while they attended schools that had limited resources with an emphasis on "Deep South" culture.

While we were there, a Tutankhamun exhibition of items from the Pharaoh's tomb was being held in Washington D.C., so it seemed like a good idea to make a trip there to expose the children to the exhibition and all of the history and treasures of the numerous museums of the Smithsonian. The exhibition was extremely popular and the crowds attending resulted in lines nearly around the block as the number of people and viewing time was restricted to allow reasonable accommodation for people to study the artifacts. (You can see I had a taste of life today many years ago!)

We kept watching museum information each day, hoping we could find a time when the lines were shorter so we would not have to spend valuable vacation time waiting. Finally, on the last afternoon of our visit, late in the day, we decided it is now or never—we will just have to stand in line.

We found a parking place on the street to the rear of the museum and started the search to find the entry line. We found a park at the end of the museum with a path through it that led to the front. The path was lined with trees and tall bushes, and in the late afternoon shadows looked rather foreboding. By staying on the sidewalk, we could stay in the open, but it was a long trek and I was in a hurry.

Although the kids and even my wife were reticent to take the shortcut, I stubbornly led us onto that route. About halfway through, we came upon a group of workers near the side of the path (remember where our kids were being schooled and who their contacts outside of our home were). Both children and my wife were tense, and even I questioned my decision because we were alone.

As we approached, one of the men called out, "Hey, come here!"

By now, even my bravado was plunging. "What's up?" I asked.

"Come here," he said again, as I edged closer. And then he asked, "Are you going to the exhibition?"

I gulped a "yes" as I cautiously approached.

"Here," he said. "I have these four tickets they gave us, and I'm not going to use them. Take them and go to the pre-ticket line. It is much shorter."

I asked if he was selling them; he emphasized "no" and refused any money.

In the pre-ticket line, there was only a few minutes wait. We had a wonderful visit to the Tutankhamun exhibit and the whole family learned a lot that day. The best and long-lasting lesson was just how thoughtful and wonderful

ALL people can be, including the African-American buildings and grounds worker, our benefactor! This is especially so now, as many people reiterate how deeply our culture has ingrained our prejudices to the degree that we don't admit so, until we experience an awakening.

Recommended TV

by Susie Baker

For your viewing ...

I highly recommend the British (originally on BBC) series "Call the Midwife" that was aired in the United States on PBS, and is now available on Netflix. The stories are based on the memoirs of Jennifer Worth, RN, RM, about her work as a midwife living and working in the East End of London during the 1950s.

It begins as Jenny arrives at Nonnatus House as a newly minted midwife. To her surprise, Nonnatus House is a convent of devoted sisters dedicated to ministering to and caring for the impoverished women of the East End. In addition to the nuns, there are several non-nun midwives like Jenny. She finds her work there personally and professionally life-affirming. At Nonnatus House, she finds dear friends and dedicated colleagues within the community of young nurses and veteran nuns.

Some of the stories are heart-wrenching as these dedicated women deal with all the emerging issues of the times, as well as problems since time immemorial, i.e., poverty, ignorance, superstition, diversity, prostitution, incest, abortion, and the list goes on, with all the elements of the human condition.

I dearly love this series (9 seasons) and can recommend it to a mature audience, male or female, guaranteeing that you will be moved, educated, and appreciative of the improvements to medical care that have occurred since the 1950s, but also impressed by the deeply personal care that the patients of that period received from the midwives.

From the Editor:

Thank you, Susie. I have been a fan of BBC television for nearly twenty years, recommending what I have liked, and getting tips from others. None has been more welcome and surprising than a suggestion from this week's essayist.

In the selection process for a new show, I have glossed over the names of hundreds of shows, including "Call the Midwife" that I wrote off thinking "no way"! That was until Susie was so enthusiastic about this show, that I decided to give it a try. Now I am hooked for the reasons she states above. This led me to conclude:

- *Avoid judging a show's worth by the title. Sometimes it captures the theme and sometimes it misses.*

- *Unless it is a bona fide turkey, do not give up on a series until the third episode.*

- *Be mindful that to last three seasons or more the show must have been well received by others. Another reason to give it a try.*

- *When watching a British TV show, especially one telling the stories of the common people, expect to miss from 30% to 50% of the words. Don't worry, if you pay attention you will not miss anything. Some people select closed captioning to get more.*

- *Having a compelling lead character is important. For me it is a key element for my enjoyment.*

Marquette Manor Foundation, Inc. was formed primarily to fund the residency cost of indigent elderly persons who reside in The Marquette Manor retirement facility. The Foundation also supports religious, musical, social, artistic, educational, recreational, and health care initiatives specially designed to benefit the residents.

We recognize that Your Good Life, a literary website that was created by Marquette residents and is offered free to seniors everywhere, is pursuing a course in keeping with the ideals we adhere to.

We applaud the efforts of Your Good Life and give our wholehearted endorsement to both the website and the book Reflections and Memories.

We extend our best wishes to you in the continuation of your great efforts.

Board of Directors
The Marquette Manor Foundation

Contributors

Susie Baker was raised on a farm in northwestern Pennsylvania and graduated from Westminster College in art education. She is a wife, mother, grandmother, and dedicated volunteer working on behalf of the Children's Hospital of Michigan. She enjoys needlework, reading, and summers in Northern Michigan. *(137)*

Federico Dies, MD, PhD, was born in France to Spanish parents. He is a Mexican physician, Mexican-American Physiologist, and husband of a beautiful Mexican girl; plus proud father of two successful sons and grandparent of two great kids. *(82, 117, 127)*

Adrienne Faist was raised on a 100-acre farm in Illinois, received a BA from Rosary College, and married a Notre Dame graduate from a nearby town. She enjoys traveling with him, their four children, and grandchildren. She also enjoys reading and hopes to leave ripples of positivity in the world. *(43)*

Barbara R. Furlow, graduated from Louisiana State University, earned a master's degree from Indiana University, and is a retired Geriatric Therapist. She was a television journalist and Feature Story Editor from the governor's mansion to the Space Center. She participates in two weekly book groups and facilitates a Contemporary Issues forum. *(106, 114)*

Sandra Hamilton graduated from The College of Mount Saint Vincent in the Bronx, New York. She spent thirty years in Westchester County, New York, and fifty-two years in Indiana. Her six children are raising families while she pursues an active life in Marquette Senior Living while assuming a leadership role in Your Good Life. *(57)*

Marion Harcourt pursued four "careers." First, in Microbiology and Biochemistry at Purdue. Second, driving five children to activities. Third, as a social worker, helping the traumatized while finding time to be a docent for Indiana Landmarks. And, finally, as a volunteer with the American Red Cross, responding to national disasters. *(61)*

Fred Hecker is a Wisconsin School of Pharmacy and Business graduate and a registered pharmacist in Wisconsin and Indiana. His working career was at Eli Lilly and Company. He enjoys traveling and has been to all seven continents. He did all this while maintaining a life-long love of the accordion. *(99)*

Beverly Carmichael Heid graduated from Indiana University with an A.B. in Economics in 1960 and an M.B.A. in Finance in 1964. She had a successful career in finance. Her hobbies include music and journalism. *(19, 34, 46, 94, 109)*

Gene Helveston, MD, is emeritus professor at Indiana University School of Medicine where he established a Pediatric Ophthalmology clinical and training service. He was later chief ophthalmologist at ORBIS, an International NGO fighting blindness worldwide, where he developed a global telemedicine consultation and teaching program. *(68)*

Joe Helveston is retired as owner/operator of a machining business and was a member of a professional chamber orchestra. He enjoys performing with a local church praise band and bell choir for Sunday services. Also, with his wife, Nancy, he plays for various entertainment venues. *(23, 40, 131)*

C. Bruce Hume graduated from Ohio State University in engineering and Butler University in business. In the Air Force, he was involved in launching intelligence satellites from Vandenburg Air Force Base. At Eli Lilly, he worked in supply and new products. He enjoys reading and travel, having visited forty countries. *(28, 64, 89)*

Contributors

Rosemary Hume has three sons and eight grandchildren. She worked at Ascension St. Vincent's Hospital in critical care nursing and human resource development. She helped plan St. Vincent Cove Spirituality Center and was director for seven years. She enjoys hiking, travel, and the study of God's creation. *(51, 66, 79, 86)*

Ruth Keenan Hillmer received a specialist in education degree (EDS) from Butler University and completed forty years in education in the Pike Township and Greenfield school systems. Her work from pre-school to administration included eighteen years teaching K–6 and eighteen years as school principal in Indiana and Illinois. *(37)*

Jacqueline King, RN, PhD, is retired from an academic career of teaching, nursing, and education. She enjoys travel, hiking, and reading primarily nonfiction. *(32, 70, 111)*

Ed Koskie is a ninety-year-old Purdue engineering graduate living in a Marquette cottage. In his senior management careers, he learned to write clearly and concisely. He and his wife of four years, Nancy, find that a late marriage can be a crowning achievement to a happy life. *(76, 102, 134)*

Patrick C. Logan, MD, is a dermatologist of fifty-one years and is still practicing. His passion is for family and his dear wife of sixty-one years. They met on a blind date while students at Notre Dame and St. Mary's College, and never looked back, He is a U.S. Navy veteran. *(48)*

Lucy Riegel is a retired CPA currently living at Marquette. She married Bob in 1961. They have four children and fifteen grandchildren. She enjoys friends and family, swimming, walking, writing, and involvement with resident issues at Marquette. Lucy's first career was running a library. Later, she transitioned to tax practice. *(84, 92)*

Margaret Hall Simpson is a retired registered nurse with expertise in hospice nursing, studying in England. She is currently moderator of the Poet's Corner, a group for poetry lovers at Marquette Senior Living and poetry editor of Your Good Life. *(54, 104, 120, 122)*

Marion R. Simpson graduated from the University of Wisconsin and is a veteran of World War II. He served in the Air Transport Command and is retired Vice President of Indiana National Bank. *(96)*

Lynda Smallwood is the Media Manager at Your Good Life, with nearly twenty years of experience in administrative and website management, including assisting in the development of an international telemedicine program for ophthalmologists. When not working, she enjoys the outdoors and spending time with family. *(125)*

Randy Trowbridge, MD, is a retired Medical Oncologist who helped establish hospice programs in Washington and Indiana. He and his wife, Alice, traveled widely, hiking and kayaking at every opportunity. During the COVID-19 pandemic he has hosted regular interactive conversations on Zoom. He enjoys reading and playing jazz guitar. *(21)*

Betty von Noorden, born in Weston Subedge, Gloucestershire, England, trained as a registered nurse, moved to Cleveland, Ohio after World War II and married a physician recently immigrated from Germany. She traveled widely helping her husband forge an eminent career in medicine. She lives in retirement in Houston, close to her daughter. *(17)*

Robert (Bob) Waeltz, CLU, is a graduate of Washington University St. Louis, and served as state of Indiana Life, Health and Financial Services manager of The Travelers Insurance Company. *(81)*

Carol Weaver, PMP, FLMI, is a retired biochemist with Dow Chemical, a Certified Project Manager and Director of Client Services for Pacific Life and One America. She enjoys paper crafting, reading, and traveling with her husband, Jim. Carol has a twin sister in Fort Wayne, Indiana. *(73)*